Mary Braithwaite

ANCIENT LUING

A historical guide to the Isle of Luing

Published by Luing History Group
Atlantic Islands Centre, Cullipool, Isle of Luing
Scotland, PA34 4TX

ISBN: 978-1-9169017-0-4

Unless otherwise indicated, all photos and maps are by the author.

Front cover drone photo: Ballycastle fort looking northwest to Ballachuan and the Isle of Mull © Iain Cruickshanks

Back cover photo: boat graffiti on north wall of Kilchattan old parish church © Mary Braithwaite

Typesetting and design by Lumphanan Press
www.lumphananpress.co.uk

Printed by Imprint Digital, UK

Contents

List of maps

Acknowledgements

Without Luing History Group and the Association of Certificated Field Archaeologists (ACFA) this book would not exist. Over two decades, Luing History Group has collected material on the island's history and people, assembled archives, surveyed the gravestones at Kilchattan, investigated a prehistoric site and organised events and activities. In 2016 we started discussions with ACFA about an archaeological walkover survey, which was carried out by ACFA and island volunteers between 2017 and 2021. In addition to the survey, transcriptions of important documents have been made, again by volunteers, notably relevant Papers of the Earls of Breadalbane (known as the Breadalbane Muniments) held at the National Records of Scotland in Edinburgh.

There are many members of Luing History Group to thank, especially past members of the Committee, islanders with good memories of Luing's recent history, and Iain Cruickshanks for drone photos. Particular thanks go to fellow Committee members Zoë Fleming, Dawn MacKenzie, Jane MacLachlan, Julia Shuff and Mary Whitmore for sharing our Group's exploits, and commenting on the book. Research for the book has involved many enjoyable days tramping across Luing, sometimes in wet and wild weather, but always with stunning views and good company. I'd especially like to thank Zoë for her knowledge of Luing's geology and digging out census data and information from our archives. Luing History Group's investigations are continuing, with a

LiDAR survey in 2020 and future plans for a coastal survey by SCAPE and a laser survey of the Kilchattan graffiti.

An immense debt is owed to ACFA and the field archaeologists who have come to Luing to undertake the survey, especially the inspirational Dugald MacInnes who has led the work. Mostly carried out in winter months when the bracken is low, ACFA's meticulous methodology has identified and recorded well over 400 features across Luing, Torsa and small neighbouring islands. The final stages of the survey and report are being completed as this book goes to press.

Specific thanks go to: John Holliday, of *An Iodhlann* on Tiree, for advice on Norse place names; to Matthew Champion, an expert on Medieval church graffiti, and Christer Westerdahl, a Norwegian expert on Medieval boats, for suggestions on aspects of the Kilchattan graffiti; and to Caroline Wickham-Jones, for friendly feedback and expertise on Scottish prehistory. Thanks also to Duncan Lockerbie of Lumphanan Press for designing and typesetting the book, and providing calm and professional publishing guidance. Finally, I'd like to thank my husband Nigel Ings for his encouragement to turn my knowledge and ideas into a book.

The background research into the history of Luing, Argyll and the Hebrides is mine. I take full responsibility for any errors of interpretation or omission, and am happy to be corrected or given additional information on the events that have influenced Luing's history.

Mary Braithwaite
August 2021

Main places on Luing mentioned in text

Introduction

Just six miles long by one-and-a-half wide, the small island of Luing is rich in historical and archaeological treasures. Prehistoric peoples built houses and monuments in stone, which are still visible today. Some were re-used in the early Medieval period, when Luing was part of the kingdom of *Dál Riata*. Then the Vikings arrived, leaving their mark on island names. Later it belonged to the Medieval Lords of the Isles, who built a chapel and used Luing's harbours for their galleys. Fleets sailed past, recorded in unique graffiti on the chapel walls. Promontory forts and lookouts were probably vital during the Medieval period to protect against invasions and clan conflict.

Luing's resources and land made it a prized possession of big landlords, yet tenant families had to work hard with little security. The island was divided into 'towns', each with several families responsible for jointly farming the land and paying rent in grain and goods. From the 17th century Luing was a hive of industry and saw major changes. Luing's three mills were busy, its townships were broken up and transformed into farmsteads, old turf and stone dykes were replaced with drystone walls, land was drained, and slate quarrying expanded. Steam boats stopped at Blackmill Bay, and Luing's population reached a peak of 860 in 1841 as roofing slates were exported around the world.

Evidence of Luing's history remains visible to this day. Some are easy to spot: the Iron Age forts, smaller duns and round houses; the slate quarries and villages at Cullipool and Toberonochy;

Kilchattan chapel and Achafolla mill; and the pier and ticket office at Blackmill Bay. Other evidence is more difficult to detect; humps and bumps in the ground or seemingly insignificant concentrations of stone.

This guide presents the story of Luing's history from ancient times to the 19th century. Numbers in brackets in the text refer to the site's number in the gazetteer at the end of the book, which presents the main sites. This book is far from the full story of Luing's past. Much research remains to be done, especially on estate documents from the 18th and 19th centuries. There are more stories to be told, particularly about Luing's families, its maritime past and the history of its townships and farms.

Key dates in Luing's history

c. 10,000 BC   Hunter-gatherers travel the islands making use of wild resources.

c. 4,000 BC   New people start arriving, bringing farming and a new Stone Age lifestyle.

c. 2,200 BC   The Bronze Age begins, introduced by a new wave of immigrants.

c. 700 BC   The Iron Age emerges and stone forts are built.

AD 400   Gaelic Kingdom of *Dál Riata* and arrival of Christianity. Kilchattan church dedicated to 6th century Irish Saint Cattan.

AD 795   Vikings attack Iona, and again in 802, 806 and 826.

AD 847   Vikings control the Isles.

890s   Norse-Pictish battle in the area of Luing, Seil and Scarba.

1090s   Expeditions by King Magnus 'Barelegs' to establish Norwegian sovereignty over the Isles.

1154	Somerled, Lord of Argyll and Kintyre, seizes the Kingdom of Man and the Isles.
1164	Somerled dies. His descendants, the Mac-Dougalls and MacDonalds, divide his vast Kingdom, the MacDougalls gaining the upper hand.
1220s–1260s	Naval expeditions by Scottish and Norwegian Kings. Boat graffiti carved on the walls of Kilchattan church.
1266	Treaty of Perth cedes control of the Hebrides to Scotland.
1309	MacDougalls defeated by Robert the Bruce and lose their lands to the MacDonalds and Campbells.
1330s–1493	MacDonalds create the Lordship of the Isles. Lands of Ardlarach are granted to the Mac-leans, great nobles of the Lordship.
1500	Control of the Isles given to the Campbell Earls of Argyll. Feuds with the Macleans. Luing invaded in 1577 & 1579.
1640s	Ravaging of Argyll by Covenanter and Royalist forces, observed by Luing poet Dorothy Brown.
1660s	Early 'Improvement': court acts control how tenants farm the land and use resources.

1690	Reformed Scottish Church settled as Presbyterian. Kilchattan church abandoned as place of worship.
1692	Netherlorn estate including Luing sold to John Campbell, Earl of Breadalbane.
1730	'Improvement' takes hold: rent increases and changes in estate management.
1751	Start of commercial slate production on Luing.
1780s	Major estate reorganisation, multi-tenant townships split into farms and crofts.
1840s	Potato famine after decades of economic decline and hardship.
1850s	Establishment of model farm and clearance of tenants at Ardluing and Kilchattan.
1870s	Resurgence of slate quarrying.
1923	Sale and breakup of Netherlorn estate following death of Earl of Breadalbane.

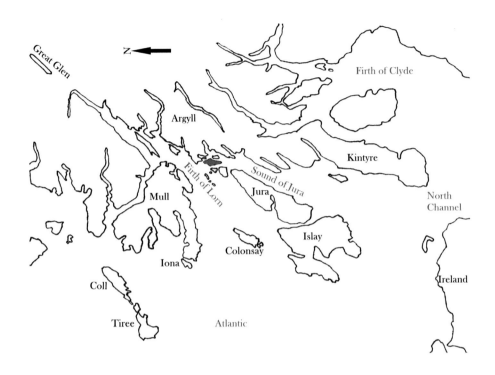

Ancient Luing

*The world of Ancient Luing was maritime and insular. Sea connected people,
clans, kings and lords. The islands were rich in resources and sea routes were
strategically important, used by prehistoric migrants from Britanny and
Vikings from Norway. Christian missionaries and Gaelic warriors sailed
to and from Ireland. Luing's harbours sheltered boats and fleets sailing the
coastal highway between the Irish Sea and the Great Glen.*

Before history: building in stone

Luing's inhabitants have made good use of its stone, a product of millions of years of prehistory. From around 750 million years ago, the supercontinent of Rodinia split apart creating a new ocean, called Iapetus. During the next 300 million years sediments accumulated on the ocean bottom, creating incredibly thick Dalradian rocks. Molten magma squeezed between layers in the sedimentary rock, forming sills. From 500 million years ago the ocean began to close, compressing and concertinaing the sedimentary rock into layers of slate, which split along cleavage planes. The sills were also altered to a hard metabasite rock, which forms the high ground in the north eastern part of Luing. Much later, around 60 million years ago, a huge volcano on Mull sent streams of magma far and wide through cracks in the slate, hardening into black basalt dykes. Between the start of the Ice Age about 2.6 million years ago and its end about 12,000 years ago, the landscape went through more transformations. Then humans started to arrive.

Between 12,000 and 6,000 years ago hunter-gatherers were exploring the Argyll coast and the Hebrides, collecting hazelnuts and wild plants, fishing and foraging the seashore, and hunting deer, boar and birds. They lived in simple camps, and moved around the islands and nearby mainland making use of seasonal resources.

Evidence of their sophisticated stone tools, fire pits and rubbish has been found on many islands around Luing, including

Woodland at Ardinamar in springtime

Jura, Islay, Mull and Colonsay, as well as around Oban bay and at
Kilmore and Kilmelford. Luing has a number of caves and rock
shelters that might have been used at this time. The ancient hazel
woodland at Ballachuan on Seil is an example of the woodland
resources used by Mesolithic peoples. Above Ardinamar bay on
Luing is a similar area of woodland, full of flowers in Spring and
hazels in Autumn.

Living with the seasons
Mesolithic people knew about climate change. Around 8,200
years ago, the climate turned colder, drier and windier in the North
Atlantic. The environment and vegetation deteriorated, making it
harder to survive and reducing the population significantly. Some
people remained, and as the climate improved the population
increased. Evidence from around 6,000 years ago suggests that a

group of Mesolithic people were moving between Oronsay, where they trapped fish and collected shellfish, and Islay, where they hunted big game. It's possible that Luing's resources were being exploited and some of the island's caves used for shelter.

Settling in

Mesolithic islanders were about to face a new challenge. Around 6,000 years ago new people started moving in, possibly from Brittany, establishing themselves alongside the resident population. Some of these new immigrants settled in our area. DNA analysis on the bones of two brothers buried at this time in an Oban cave link them to Brittany. The lifestyle of the migrants was very different to indigenous groups. Instead of moving with the seasons and living with few material possessions, a more settled life emerged. Land was farmed, animals were raised and pottery was produced and used. Great stone monuments were built, often aligned on seasonal movements of the sun. Although their tools were made from stone, they had impressive artistic and architectural skills and an interest in astronomy and ritual. Argyll abounds with Neolithic stone circles, standing stones, burial cairns, chambered tombs and rock art, especially in and around Kilmartin Glen. On the nearby island of Shuna to the east of Luing are the remains of a Neolithic chambered tomb.

On Luing there are few clues to this period. Some worked flints including a partly-made arrowhead, found in 2021 on the hill above Cuan, indicate the presence of people at some point in early prehistory. Flint was their preferred stone for tools, but is not local and would have been a valuable

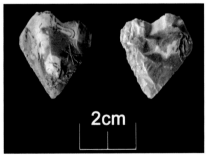

Flint arrowhead blank from Cuan
(Courtesy: Dugald MacInnes, ACFA)

commodity in those days. There may be the fallen remains of two standing stones, one north of Ardlarach, the other south of Park. More convincing evidence is a large slate boulder carved with cup marks, incorporated in the entrance of the later prehistoric dun at Leccamore. Cup marks are typical of late Neolithic and early Bronze Age art, and the slate is local. The artist or artists may well have lived on Luing, its fertile land almost certainly supporting a small population of farming families at this time.

The Age of Bronze

About 4,200 years ago, a new culture and social dynamic spread across Britain, probably introduced by another wave of new immigrants. While some traditions continued, new practices were introduced, including individual burials, round houses, and the use of copper and bronze to make tools, ornaments and weapons. The Bronze Age, which lasted in Scotland for nearly 1,500 years until around 700 BC, was a period of international trade and cultural contacts that linked Atlantic Scotland with the Mediterranean.

On Luing some of the round houses recorded during the archaeological survey may date to the late Bronze Age. Below Ballycastle fort at Ardinamar are four circular structures, possibly roundhouses (11). On the same ridge to south are the foundations of another well-built round house (14). Not far away at Park is an 11m diameter circle of boulders (44), which may once have been a late Bronze Age house.

Other evidence suggests that on the ridge of metabasite rock at Ardinamar was a late Bronze Age farming settlement. Between Ballycastle fort and the well-built round house are stretches of low stone banks forming small fields associated with small stone structures, similar to late Bronze Age sites on Islay and Arran and elsewhere in Scotland. To the north and north-east of Bal-lycastle fort are more fragments of small stone-walled fields and

Largest stone circle below Ballycastle fort

Roundhouse in foreground, view north to Ballycastle fort

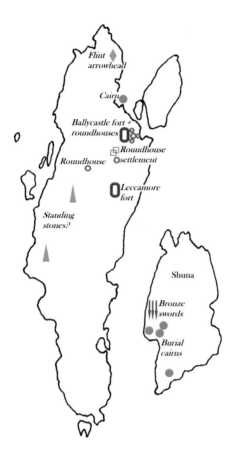

Prehistoric Luing and Shuna

Some of Luing's most prominent sites date to the later prehistoric period. Neolithic people buried their dead in a chambered cairn on Shuna and carved cup marks on a slate boulder, which was set in the entrance of Leccamore fort in the Iron Age. Shuna continued to be used for burials and rituals in the Bronze Age, a spectacular deposit of three bronze swords marking a special event. Roundhouse settlements and an intertidal cairn were built on Luing, and in the Iron Age two impressive stone forts were constructed on a prominent ridge, visible from afar.

a small cellular structure, as well as several 'clearance cairns' – circular piles of rocks cleared from the land in order to facilitate the cultivation of crops – their size and shape suggesting that they too may date from this period.

Burials continued on Shuna, not in a chambered tomb but in 'kerb cairns', circular stone mounds with large kerbstones around their perimeter. The remains of three kerb cairns survive at the southern end of Shuna. This area seems to have had special significance for local communities. At the end of the Bronze Age – between 950 and 750 BC – three bronze swords were buried close to the cairns, their points sticking vertically downwards. They were found in 1875 during the digging of a ditch in peat. The deliberate burial of such rich items must have marked an occasion of great importance. The reasons will never be known, but profound changes were occurring that affected the lifestyles and livelihoods of people in the region.

Around 700 BC the Bronze Age came to a close in Atlantic Scotland, associated with environmental and climatic changes,

Cairn on Sgeir Carnaich (Courtesy: Chris Whitmore)

the end of the international trade in bronze and the introduction of iron. Around this time on Luing a large stone cairn was in use on the tidal islet of Sgeir Carnaich (9), at the southern end of the maritime haven between Luing and Torsa. The cairn was built on top of a slate outcrop using metabasite stone, the nearest source being the Ardinamar ridge close by, with its possible late Bronze Age farming settlement. Embedded in the cairn were timbers, some of which were removed many years ago. Luckily one oak timber remained when the cairn was investigated in 2009; carbon-dating of the timber produced a calibrated date of 780-500 BC, the transition between the late Bronze and Iron Ages. When the cairn was in use, timbers might have stood as upright posts. Deposits overlying the oak timber contained red oxidised clay, animal teeth, shells, fragments of charcoal and possible fire-cracked stones, suggesting fires and feasting.

It's at this time that islet dwellings – crannogs – were starting to be constructed in lochs and inter-tidal estuaries in Argyll. Many were lived on, large enough for a homestead and activities such as grain processing, cooking and weaving. Other functions are likely, including as markers, beacons or places for rituals and ceremonies. There was a reverence for water, with rich objects deposited in watery places (as the bronze swords were on Shuna). Intertidal zones between sea and land, particularly those close to maritime trading routes and resources, seem to have been especially important. Whatever its purpose, Sgeir Carnaich was part of a trend of round monumental architecture in conspicuous locations, constructed by communities keen to demonstrate their presence.

The Iron Age

Some of Luing's most impressive stone monuments were constructed during the Iron Age, built so robustly they survive to this day. Two stunning hill top forts – Ballycastle and Leccamore

– are the most visible of Luing's late prehistoric buildings. Round houses and circular enclosures continued to be used, possibly including those on the eastern slopes of Ballycastle fort (11). Pastoralism became more prevalent in the Iron Age and cattle an important source of wealth. Quern stones found at Leccamore show people grew and milled cereals, most probably barley, while animal bones and sea shells indicate stock-raising (sheep, cattle and pigs), hunting of wild animals and inshore fishing.

Luing's late prehistoric inhabitants were farmers and seafarers, travelling by sea and using marine resources. No prehistoric boats have yet been found in the Hebrides but finds elsewhere in Scotland suggest that long logboats constructed from oak might have been in use for inland travel and some sort of hide-covered vessel for sea voyages.

Luing's Iron Age forts

Ballycastle and Leccamore forts are located on a long ridge of metabasite rock running south from Ardinamar; Ballycastle at the northern end (11), Leccamore at the southern end (17). Locally called forts, they are classified in archaeological terminology as 'duns', 'complex Atlantic roundhouses' or in the case of Ballycastle as a 'dun enclosure'. Making sense of the great variety of monumental stone enclosures constructed in the Iron Age has occupied archaeologists for decades, and there is still no agreement on a system of classification. Luing's forts were first described in the late 19th century, in a survey of duns and forts in Netherlorn and Nether Lochaber. Parts of Leccamore fort were excavated in the 1890s, but there have been no excavations at Ballycastle.

LECCAMORE FORT

Leccamore is a 'galleried dun', with intramural galleries and a stairway set in a substantial stone wall. The 4-5m thick wall encloses an oval area roughly 20m by 13m. It has two entrances, in the southwest and northeast. Outside the northern entrance are two deep rock-cut ditches separated by a steep, rocky outcrop, protecting the dun at its weakest defensive point.

Leccamore Fort from the air (Courtesy: Iain Cruickshanks)

During initial excavations in 1890 the southern entrance, which was filled with fallen stones, slates and earth, was cleared out. Originally it was a roofed and paved passage barred by a door, with vertical jamb stones and deep bar holes. The vertical jamb stone on the eastern side of the passage is made from slate and has at least fifteen circular indentations – cup-marks – cut into its inner face in two parallel lines, which are typical of late Neolithic and early Bronze Age art.

Slate with cup marks in Leccamore Fort entrance
(Courtesy: Dugald MacInnes, ACFA)

Subsequent excavations in 1892 explored the smaller northern entrance and an adjacent area of the interior. The excavations exposed several internal features. A scarcement or ledge of rough masonry was identified against the western interior wall of the dun, which might indicate that lean-to buildings were built against the wall. At the northern entrance a small intramural gallery was found off the eastern side and, on the western side, a larger, corbelled intramural gallery that might have been a guard cell, with steps leading upwards to the top of the dun wall.

The objects found at Leccamore fort during these 19th century excavations included stone discs and pounders, rotary querns, a bronze stem, a fragment of an iron blade, a piece of iron slag, a quantity of wild and domesticated animal bones (red deer, roe deer, pig, ox and seal), sea shells and charcoal. This assemblage of objects is typical of many Iron Age sites in Argyll and does not enable a precise date for the fort's construction and use. The presence of rotary querns – which were a major improvement on the earlier saddle querns – could indicate a date after c.200 BC, although recent studies suggest they may have been introduced into Scotland as early as the 4th or 5th century BC. Excavations of duns elsewhere in Argyll suggest that they were being constructed no earlier than the 4th century BC.

One special object was found at Leccamore, the upper and lower stones of a miniature rotary quern, c.13cm in diameter. The miniature quern stones probably date to the early centuries AD (the Roman Iron Age), and are the only examples found so far in western Scotland, other examples being clustered in eastern Scotland with a few in the north. They could not have been used for grain, but may have been used to grind small quantities of seeds, herbs or minerals, perhaps for the preparation of pigments, drugs or medicines.

The other object of interest is an early Medieval bone pin, found with a sawn piece of antler and associated with a hearth in the southern entrance passage. This pin dates activity at Leccamore to the later 1st millennium AD, when Argyll was at the heart of the kingdom of *Dál Riata*. Re-use of an Iron Age site was not unusual, with duns, brochs, forts and crannogs often showing evidence of use during the early Medieval period.

BALLYCASTLE FORT

Ballycastle, the impressive hill-top fort at Ardinamar, may once have been called *Dùnedin*, a name now associated with a nearby, but much later, croft. Like Leccamore, it is oval in shape but substantially bigger, 32m by 18m internally with a 4m thick enclosing

Ballycastle fort looking east to mainland (Courtesy: Iain Cruickshanks)

wall, which even now is 2m high in places. It is classified as a dun, or as a 'dun enclosure' because of its size as it is too large to have been roofed. Features inside the fort, including an oval-shaped bank of stone and a possible cistern, may be evidence of internal buildings.

Although stones are reported to have been taken from the site for building later walls and farm buildings, a remarkable amount remains, suggesting that the wall might originally have been 3m high. Variations in masonry style might indicate different phases of construction and re-building. A curve of boulders extending beyond the base of the fort wall on its southern side suggests there might even have been an earlier structure.

The fort had one entrance on its eastern side, which could be closed with a door, the bar hole on the north side still visible. Outside the entrance is a curve of walling, which has been interpreted as a 'protective screen' to the door and entrance passage. A gap in the wall on the west post-dates the fort. Unlike Leccamore there appear to have been no intramural cells or stairs, although these features were not visible at Leccamore prior to the excavations.

Immediately below Ballycastle, on the eastern flanks of the hill, are four circular stone structures. Three of them may have been small round houses. The largest of the four circles may have been a house or possibly an enclosure for animals. The remains of cross-walls running between outcrops are visible below the fort entrance, possibly controlling access to the fort. On the north side are small platforms or enclosures, again suggesting that activities took place outside the fort's walls.

Iron Age settlement and society on Luing

What were Ballycastle and Leccamore used for when they were built in the Iron Age? Duns and forts used to be seen as the fortified houses of ruling chiefs and nobles, at the top end of a hierarchy of Iron Age settlements, with the majority of people living in small round houses. Recent analyses have led to significant reinterpretations of the dating and possible functions of Iron Age forts and duns, and to society at that time.

Simple roundhouses started to be constructed in the late Bronze Age, and continued to be used in the Iron Age. From around 400 BC Iron Age communities in Argyll started to construct more monumental forms of dry-stone architecture, including duns and forts. The relationship between the small houses and large buildings is unclear, both chronologically and in terms of function. On Luing, all but one of the identifiable simple stone roundhouses are located within close proximity of Ballycastle and Leccamore forts, the exception being just three-quarters of a mile away.

While some duns may have been the permanent dwellings of individual households or extended families, others may have been used seasonally or episodically for special or communal activities, such as iron or craft production, feasting or social events. The placing in the entrance of Leccamore of a cup-marked slate boulder decorated by past inhabitants – perhaps 2,000 years or more previously – was not untypical of Iron Age practices, perhaps symbolising past generations and traditions. The quern stones, hammerstones and quantities of animal and fish bones found at Leccamore could be the result of communal feasting, while the iron slag suggests metalworking somewhere in the vicinity. Communal feasts associated with metalworking are known from other Iron Age sites in Scotland, such as the Cairns broch in Orkney where a huge feast accompanied by alcoholic beverage took place around AD 300.

Significant labour and conscious planning were deployed in the construction of Ballycastle and Leccamore. Their location and scale meant they were highly visible in the wider landscape, notably so in the case of Ballycastle which can still be seen from the sound of Luing to the west and the mainland to the east. Furthermore, their architecture and design created a marked boundary between the world outside and that within, the people and activities within hidden from those outside, and vice versa.

In the absence of excavation and detailed chronology, the relationship between the two forts is unknown. It is not impossible that they were in use at the same time by local communities, but with different functions. If constructed at different times, the earlier structure was evidently not destroyed when the later one was built. Resource-rich local communities may have been capable of deploying the labour required to construct them over many years or several generations. Iron Age communities at this period appear not to have invested in individual or portable material culture but rather in monumental architecture and in rituals associated with feasting and craft activities. It is possible that the forts on Luing were used for important collective and symbolic activities such as feasts, festivals and marriage alliances, and not for permanent habitation by one family. At times of threat, they may also have provided a refuge for the local community.

Iron Age society in Scotland, at least in the Early to Middle period, seems not to have been hierarchical. Power and decision-making were more widely shared and might have varied according to circumstance. However, natural resources were being used more intensively and there was extensive deforestation, which may have led to environmental stress and significant impacts on Iron Age society. The social structures of the early and middle part of the Iron Age could not be sustained, and new forms and expressions of elite power were emerging. By the end of the Iron Age, hierarchical societies were developing, their names recorded by Roman geographers and writers.

Dál Riata and early Christianity

When Ptolemy, the Roman geographer, mapped the peoples of northern Britain around AD 150 Luing appears to have belonged to the *Epidii*, whose islands were called the *Ebudae*, after which the Hebrides were named.

By the 5th century AD the territory of the *Epidii* formed the core of *Dál Riata*, a Gaelic-speaking Christian kingdom with territory on both sides of the North Channel. In the far north of Ireland there was a royal centre at Dunseverick and an ecclesiastical centre at Armoy. In Scotland *Dál Riata* stretched from Arran and Kintyre in the south to at least Morvern in the north, encompassing the islands in between, including Mull, Islay, Jura, Colonsay and Luing. There were royal sites at Dunadd and Dunollie, and the leading ecclesiastical site for *Dál Riata* as a whole was Iona.

Dál Riata was probably not a unitary kingdom in the way that we might understand it, though at times it was ruled by a single overking. It was composed of several powerful dynasties, each dynasty – *cenél* – linked by a network of kinship ties and a common ancestor. *Cenél nGabráin,* who dominated *Dál Riata* for much of the time, were based in Kintyre and Arran. Their dominance was challenged around the turn of the 7th and 8th centuries by the *Cenél Loairn*, who gave their name to Lorn and whose centre of power was Dunollie. Other *cenéla* were the *Cenél nOengusa* centred on Islay and *Cenél Comgaill,* after whom Cowal was named. At the centre of *Dál Riata* was Dunadd, a place of

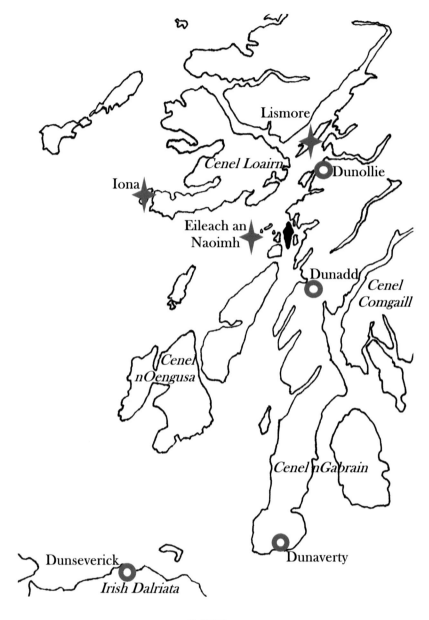

Dál Riata

Dál Riata's main kin groups (Cenél) and important Christian and royal sites

power, royal ceremony, international trade and the production of fine metalwork and jewellery.

Luing lay in the area of the *Cenél Loairn* and on the sea routes between Dunollie and Dunadd. Close by were important religious sites established in the 6th century AD by Irish missionaries on Iona, Lismore and Eileach an Naoimh in the Garvellachs.

Dál Riata was a maritime kingdom, with many islands and peninsulas. Travel by sea was the easiest means of moving any distance. Currachs, made of wicker and cowhide, were probably the most common seagoing craft. Saint Columba is said to have used a currach. St Beccan of Rùm, who lived on Iona from 632–677, described a voyage of Columba:

> *In scores of curraghs with an army of wretches he crossed*
> *   the long-haired sea.*
> *He crossed the wave-strewn wild region,*
> *Foam flecked, seal-filled, savage, bounding, seething, white-*
> *   tipped, pleasing, doleful.*

Historical sources also mention large timber ships, called "long ships", perhaps similar to later Viking ships. Some might have been used for long-distance trade. Excavations at Dunadd found material from the Mediterranean and fragments of glass and pottery from France, indicating the trading connections of *Dál Riatan* elite at this period. Control of trade was one of their sources of power and wealth. Ships were also important for less peaceful purposes. Attacks by Picts and Northumbrians, and internal conflicts between *Cenél*, are known to have taken place. Irish Annals record that Dunollie was attacked three times – in AD 686, 698, and 701 – probably during conflicts between *Cenél*. It was rebuilt in AD 714 by *Dál Riatan* King Selbach mac Ferchair (d. 730), who had destroyed the stronghold in AD 701.

Dál Riata had a large war fleet manned by skilled sailors, capable of undertaking far-reaching sea expeditions. It had an organised system for creating the fleet. An important 7th century document called the *Senchus fer nAlban* contains a naval and military survey of the *Dál Riatan Cenél*. It lists the 'houses' (*tech*) in each *Cenél* and their obligations to provide boats and warriors. Every twenty houses had to provide two seven-bench boats and 28 oarsmen. *Cenél Loairn* had 430 'houses', and had to provide 21 boats and 700 fighters for sea expeditions. There has been much debate about the nature of a 'house', but it is thought that it may have corresponded to an extended family.

As well as providing military and naval support, households would have contributed food, labour and hospitality to their chief or lord, who in return provided protection and access to land and resources. The chief or lord's overall control of land, and ability to place kinspeople and followers on this land, was an essential underpinning of power within *Dál Riata*.

Luing is not mentioned in the fragments that survive of *Dál Riatan* history, but it must have been an important island of the *Cenél Loairn* given its rich agricultural land, proximity to major sites and sea routes, and maritime havens. The 19th century excavations at Leccamore fort found a bone pin dating to the later 1st millennium AD, indicating that it was re-used during the *Dál Riatan* period (17). The bone pin was found in the southern entrance passage together with a short length of sawn antler bone, both associated with a hearth. As the interior of the fort was not investigated, it's not clear if the fort was used occasionally (perhaps by someone keeping warm and making bone tools while they kept watch) or had become the imposing homestead of a Cenél Loairn family. Its location close to arable land, a safe harbour and an early Christian chapel is typical of important settlements at this period.

It's not impossible that other sites on Luing date to this period. Islet sites or crannogs re-emerge as locations for settlements in the early Historic period, in Scotland and in Ireland, where they are typically dated to the second half of the 1st millennium AD. In Loch Seil, close to Luing, is a crannog site, which produced a calibrated date of AD 430-650 from alder wood. This was an artificial island with a roughly rectangular stone-built platform surrounded by a stone revetment wall and with a possible docking area for a boat. A candidate for a site on Luing might be the island 'dun' in the large bay on the east side of Ardluing (28).

Kilchattan and the arrival of Christianity
In the 5th century AD, Ireland was being converted to Christianity by the missionary Patrick (521-597). He baptised thousands of people, ordained priests to lead new Christian communities, and converted the sons of kings and wealthy women, some of whom became nuns. Missionaries set sail and established monasteries throughout the Hebrides and western seaboard. One of the earliest was Eileach an Naoimh, at the south end of the Garvellachs and within sight of Luing, said to have been founded in AD 542 by Brendan of Clonfert (484-577). The two beehive cells there are similar to early monastic sites in Co. Kerry, Ireland. The smaller island to the north is known as Brendan's retreat, and there are many dedications to Brendan in the area, including Kilbrandon on Seil. Brendan is famous for his legendary journey in search of the Isle of the Blessed. Later in life he returned to Ireland.

In AD 563 Columba travelled to Scotland with a dozen followers and established a monastery on Iona, which had been granted to him by a kinsman Conall mac Comgaill King of *Dál Riata*. Iona was well located for travel between Ireland and Scotland, and within easy reach of Pictland, Strathclyde and Northumbria, which were other important territories at this time. Columba was an aristocrat by background and an influential and important leader of a new religion. Iona was often crowded and noisy, and Columba frequently left for a place known as Hinba to escape the

Beehive cells on Eileach an Naoimh

throng and meditate in peace. Various remote places have been suggested for Hinba, but a good candidate is Eileach an Naoimh. Columba's mother Eithne is said to have been buried there, and as an old man Brendan visited Columba on Hinba.

Many early churches on and near Luing are dedicated to Irish saints. Kilbride on Seil is dedicated to Brigid, who is said to have been baptised by Patrick. Kilchattan on Luing is dedicated to Cattan, an Irish monk active in the 6th century, who may – like Columba – have been connected to *Dál Riatan* royalty. Churches dedicated to Cattan can be found on Bute, where he is said to have finally settled, as well as Colonsay, Gigha, Islay and Lismore.

The old parish church at Kilchattan (24) was built in the late 12th century AD, but there may have been worship at this site for several centuries before this. The church sits on an elevated area of ground, possibly hiding earlier buildings. Sites with names prefixed by 'Kil' indicate an early ecclesiastical settlement or burial ground, possibly dating to the sixth to tenth centuries.

Early Christian sites tend to be located near fertile land in strategic locations, and sometimes close to holy wells. Toberonochy means 'Duncan's well', though it is not known if it had any religious significance. Kilchattan Bay, which the chapel overlooks, would have been an important maritime haven for travellers by sea at this early period, as in later times (27).

Cross carved on stone in west wall of Kilchattan church

Another possible clue to an early date for Kilchattan is a carving of a cross on a large stone set low in the external west-facing wall of the church. It has some similarities to early crosses at Kilmory Oib and Eilean Mor, near Loch Sween in the Sound of Jura, dated to the 8th or 9th centuries AD. The stone may have originally belonged to an earlier chapel or burial ground at Kilchattan.

Rise and fall of Dál Riata

Dál Riata was at its height in the 6th and 7th centuries AD. Monasteries and chapels spread Christianity across the Kingdom and beyond to Pictland and Northumbria. Iona was at the centre of a major monastic system in Britain and Ireland, renowned for its scriptorium which produced important and beautiful documents. Skilled craftspeople made elaborately carved crosses and fine metalwork and jewelry. Naval expeditions took fleets and warriors to Orkney and the Isle of Man, and there were attacks on rival kingdoms in Strathclyde and Northumberland.

By the 8th century AD, *Dál Riata*'s golden age was coming to an end and there were military defeats. In AD 736 the royal site of Dunadd was captured by Angus King of the Picts. Five years later the Picts 'hammered' *Dál Riata,* bringing it under Pictish overlordship. There were unsuccessful attempts to challenge Pictish authority, including a battle in AD 789, and soon after *Dal Riata*'s population faced a new threat. Vikings attacked Iona in AD 795 along with Rathlin island off the northern Irish coast. These early 'hit and run' raids were carried out by small groups of Norwegian Vikings looking for portable wealth, particularly fine metalwork from ecclesiastical sites.

Dál Riata was fragmenting, from internal conflict and external threats. Iona was attacked again by Vikings in AD 802, 806 and 826. The last known King of *Dál Riata*, Áed mac Boanta, died in Pictland – alongside the King of the Picts and numerous others – in a disastrous battle against Vikings in AD 839. By this time the attackers were no longer mere raiders, but Scandinavian leaders with substantial fleets and mercenary armies. Their aims were to control strategic areas and exact taxes and tribute, thus obtaining goods, cattle and people to sell in the markets of Dublin and elsewhere. It's possible the fleets and maritime skills of *Dál Riata* were also sought by the Vikings, to complement and strengthen their own naval and military resources.

Dál Riata lost control of its islands, which became the *Suðrøyjar* (Innse Gall in Gaelic, appropriately Islands of the Foreigners), while the mainland became known as Airer Gaedel (Coastline of the Gael), from which Argyll is named. There was another loss in AD 849 when the relics of St Columba were moved from Iona. Some went to Ireland, where many of Iona's monks had gone, taking their richly-decorated manuscripts with them. Other Columban relics were moved by Cinaed mac Alpín, King of the Picts, to Dunkeld, which became the leading church and bishopric of Pictland.

By the 10th century AD *Dál Riata* had disappeared as a Kingdom and the royal site of Dunollie was abandoned. Power had shifted decisively to Pictland, whose Kings were forging a new identity that included claims of descent from the Kings of *Dál Riata* and adoption of its ecclesiastical traditions and Gaelic language. Some have claimed the *Cenél Loairn* dynasty survived by moving through the Great Glen to Moray (with MacBeth its most famous son). However, environmental evidence does not suggest a major decline in population or intensity of land use in Lorn, and indeed there was significant deforestation around the turn of the millennium, suggesting that the local population was numerous enough to impact the environment.

Similarities between circular homesteads dated to this period in Perthshire and Argyll and two structures on Luing could indicate that island life continued. A substantial stone-walled circular structure at Ardinamar (13) and a large circular stone and turf structure at Park (45) match descriptions of Medieval fortified homesteads found in NW Perthshire and Argyll; they are often sited on low knolls or bluffs but not in easily-defensible positions, have walls no more than 1.5m high, are close to later settlements and communication routes, and appear to be associated with pastoralism. Dating evidence places them in the late 1st millennium AD. It has been suggested that the fortified homesteads in

Perthshire belonged to Gaelic-speaking Scots of *Dál Riata* who moved out of their Argyll homeland as a result of displacement by Norse settlers. Perhaps the fortified homesteads on Luing belonged to islanders who remained after the Norse arrived.

Circular structure at Park looking west

Possible fortified homestead at Ardinamar

Vikings to Lords of the Isles

By 847 Vikings occupied the southern Hebrides, the start of nearly 400 years of Norse control. Thanks to Irish and other Annals, we know something of what happened at this time. The early decades were dominated by the powerful brothers Olaf and Ímar, who founded Viking Dublin and conducted raids far and wide, possibly from an inner Hebridean base. During the 860s and 870s they targeted Pictland, and in 870 the Brittonic Kingdom of Alt Clut was attacked. After a four-month siege of its capital at Dumbarton Rock, a host of Britons, Picts, Scots and Northumbrians were carried away in a fleet of 200 boats to be sold as slaves in Dublin. There are suggestions of a Pictish-Norse pact, whereby territory in the former *Dál Riata* was exchanged for protection from attack elsewhere, and a marriage alliance between a Pictish princess and an Irish High King that may also have been aimed at limiting Norse attacks. A few years later, during an attempt to gain tribute from the Picts, Olaf was killed by King Causintín, who himself died at Norse hands in 875-6.

In the 890s the conflict reached Luing itself, a battle taking place at '*innisibsolian*', argued to be the islands of Seil, Luing and Scarba, which was won by the Picts. A memory of Norse period battles may be contained in a local folk legend of a battle between Scots and Danes at Craignish on the nearby mainland, which resulted in a win for the Scots and the slaying of 'Danish King Olaf'. Close by is the 'field of the bay of the heads' suggesting a significant loss of life. True or not, Luing's position – at the

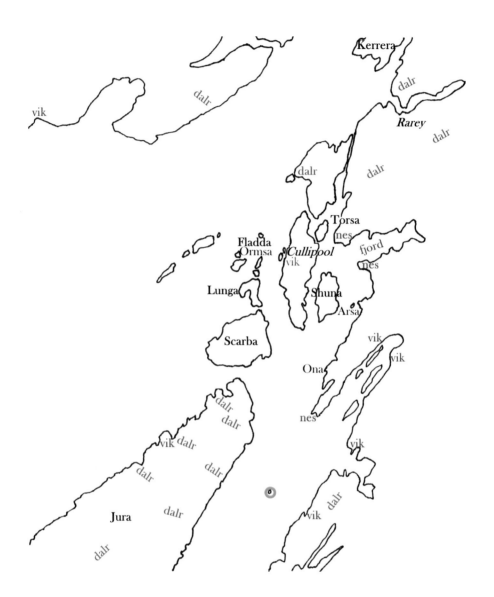

Norse place names around Luing

*Norse place names record the occupation of headlands (nes), bays (vik) and
valleys (dalr), and the use of sea inlets (fjord) and islands. Many Norse island
names survive around Luing, on which Kulli established a farm. In the Sound
of Jura a gold arm ring of a Viking leader was lost in the 10th century.*

boundary between Innse Gall and Airer Gaedel and on the main route from the Viking Irish Sea to Pictland through the Great Glen – must have made it vulnerable.

Place-name evidence shows that the Norse achieved widespread control of the islands and coastal areas of the mainland around Luing. Luing itself (*Luyng* or *Loyng* in early documents) has been

Vikings *were sea raiders from southern Scandinavia. Viking may originally have meant those making long sea journeys, but came to be associated with Norse raiders and plunderers. The thrilling Orkneyinga Saga – part fact, part fiction – recounts how the 11th century Earls Rognvald and Thorfinn would spend quiet winters in Orkney, and every summer go raiding, laying waste the Welsh, Irish and Scots 'with fire and flame'. If other Vikings encroached on their territory, they were quick to repulse them with full military force.*

*Not all **Norse** were Vikings. Some came to farm and fish, others were craftspeople and traders, though trading included slaves and stolen goods. Some were rich and powerful leaders, for whom summer raiding was a part-time activity. Earl Thorfinn the Mighty ruled Orkney and controlled large areas of northern Scotland and the Hebrides. He was the son of a Norse Earl and a daughter of a King of the Scots, grew up in the Scottish court, paid allegiance to the Norwegian King and made a pilgrimage to Rome. While the early Viking raiders were pagans, the later Norse were Christians, firmly established in many areas of Scotland.*

suggested as Norse, from *lyng* (heather) or *long* (ship), although an earlier, pre-Celtic origin is also considered possible. Around Luing are many islands with Norse names – Torsa, Shuna, Lunga, Scarba to name a few ('*ay*' is Old Norse for island). Topographical place names – such as *vik*, *nes* and *dalr* for bay, headland and valley – are widely accepted as indicating the earliest phases of Norse settlement. Many can still be identified on the islands and mainland around Luing, surviving long after abandonment of the Norse language, often absorbed into later Gaelic names.

From the pattern of names, it seems the early Norse settlers were keen to occupy strategically-sited headlands and islands on major sea routes and close to sheltered harbours and sea lochs. Immediately east of Luing on the mainland coast are three head-lands with *nes* names (Degnish, Asknish and Craignish). Degnish and Asknish lie either side of the entrance to a *fjord* (*melphord* in a 17th century document, Melfort today). The headland of Craignish to the south lies close to three bays with *vik* names, where fleets of longboats could have been drawn up. Within sight of all three *nes* is the island of Shuna, possibly from the Norse *Sjónar-ey* 'watch island'. The occupation of headlands and small off-shore islands has been suggested as the first phase of Norse settlement on Orkney, and a similar process may have taken place here. This arrangement of headlands and bays may be the Hebridean equivalent of the *longphort* (ship harbours) in Ireland, which were constructed in the 830-840s as bases for Viking raiding. *Longphort* were large fortified areas, often at the confluence of an estuary and tributary river, giving direct access to the sea and providing protection for fleets and forces. The Norse took no chances when it came to controlling sea-lanes and protecting their fleets and forces.

A significant number of valley – *dalr* – names also survive around Luing, notably on Jura and around the Firth of Lorn. Valleys provided access to valuable resources such as wood and pasture. Wool, meat and skins were important commodities, and pasture was needed for cattle captured during raids or obtained as tribute. Timber and wool were required for making and mending boats and their huge sails. Almost all of the *dalr* names are valleys with direct access to and from the sea, in close proximity to the Sound of Jura and Firth of Lorn, both major routes. They are also close to Colonsay and Islay, from where raids may have been launched on lands to the south and east. The concentration of rich Viking graves dating to the period 850-950 on west Islay, Colonsay and Oronsay, including rich female burials and a spectacular boat grave of a leader at Kiloran Bay, indicates an area of prosperity and power, and the maintenance of a strong Scandinavian identity.

Raiding and warfare continued into the tenth century. Although the powerful Dublin dynasty was in control, this did not always bring peace to the Hebrides. While strong kings, such as Olaf Guthfrithsson and his cousin Olaf Cuarán, could bring all the island and mainland territories under their rule, at other times there were challenges from within and outside the dynasty. The 970s and 980s were particularly troubled. For a time Maccus Haraldsson, based on the Isle of Man, was 'king of Man and the Hebrides' according to a Welsh Chronicle. The presence of Maccus Haraldsson alongside the King of Scots and King of Strathclyde at a meeting called by King Edgar of the English in Chester in 973 shows that Hebridean Kings were major players.

The Battle of Tara in 980, won resoundingly by the Irish against Olaf Cuarán and his Hebridean forces, had major repercussions well beyond Ireland. Olaf Cuarán retired *'in penitence and pilgrimage'* to Iona, where he died the following year. Almost 200 years had passed since the first Norse attacks, and the Norse were well established in the Hebrides. Like his compatriots, Olaf was a Christian. He had Gaelic poets in his retinue and was probably bilingual. He married daughters of Irish Kings. The

Norse dominated local and regional politics, and made major contributions to economic, cultural and religious life. Crosses and grave-slabs at Iona and Port Ellen on Islay were carved with Christian and Norse decoration, a sign that Gaelic and Norse traditions were starting to merge.

The defeat at Tara and Olaf's death on Iona brought a renewed period of strife, Olaf's sons fighting each other for dominance and opening the region up to other contenders. There were attacks by Earl Sigurd II from Orkney, perhaps in alliance with the Haraldsson brothers from the Isle of Man, and by the Norwegian prince Olaf Tryggvesson, who later became King of Norway. Gofraid Haraldsson in particular profited from the disruption. It's perhaps in the course of an attack that a gold arm ring was lost overboard close to Luing in the Sound of Jura (these days it's on display at the National Museum of Scotland). A similar arm ring was deposited in a hoard around 975 at Ballaquayle on the Isle of Man. Gold arm rings were given to military leaders of Norse kings, as a praise poem to King Harald reveals:

By their clothing, their gold armlets,
You see they are the king's friends.
They bear red cloaks, stained shields,
Silver-clad swords, ringed mailcoats,
Gilded sword-belts, engraved helmets,
Rings on their arms, as Harald gave them.

Gold Viking armring from
Sound of Jura (Courtesy:
National Museums Scotland)

Iona was attacked at Christmas 986, probably targeted for its political significance as well as its wealth, indicated by a hoard of silver coins and other objects buried there around 985. The group responsible for the attack had their come-uppance the following year, the Annals of Ulster reporting *'A great slaughter of the Danes who plundered Í, and three score and three hundred of them were slain'*. In 989 the same Annals reported the death in Irish Dal Riata of Gofraid Haraldsson 'King of the Hebrides', the first surviving reference to a *Ri Innsi Gall*. Gofraid's son Ragnall was also accorded this title at his death in 1005. By the turn of the millennium the Norse-Gaelic Kingdom of Man and the Isles had emerged, to which Luing belonged. Two expeditions by King Magnus 'Barelegs' of Norway in the 1090s established Norwegian control over the islands, which continued – at least formally – until the 13th century.

Despite this long history of Viking raiders and Norse kingdoms in the vicinity of Luing, no archaeological evidence of their settlements has yet been found. Some of the place name evidence indicates later Norse settlement, notably Cullipool (Kulli's farm). Cullipool is the only surviving 'habitative' place name in our area. As a *'bolstadr'* name (pool or pol = *bol*) it is supposed to be later in date than the *vik, dalr* and *nes* names. And *bol* names are generally thought to indicate a secondary settlement, created by splitting a larger and earlier farm. An expert on Norse names in the Hebrides has suggested that Bardrishaig (Ardrysack in its earliest form) could be a Gaelicised Norse name, *Hrísvík* or *Hríshagi* 'inlet or pasture of the brush woodland' (8). If this was the name of a Norse farm, it may later have been split, part becoming Kulli's farm. Torsa may also be a later Norse settlement, from old Norse Þórisey or Þórðsey (Þórir's island), and may have been a fishing station. The Norse had stronger boats, a new fishing technology with long lines and were newly exploiting deep-water fishing grounds.

It is possible that few Norse families settled in the area. The Norse leaders may have established military and political control without significant migration, no doubt exploiting island inhabitants and slaves for labour and marrying into local families. Willingly or unwillingly, men from the Hebrides fought alongside Vikings in Ireland. Analysis of the skeletons of two young men buried in early Viking Dublin showed that they were born in western Scotland, confirming historical evidence of Gaels amongst Viking forces. DNA evidence shows that Norse ancestry is very low in Argyll (and in the Isle of Man and Ireland) compared to much higher levels in the Western and Northern Isles.

Archaeological evidence for Norse settlement may yet be found, though different from the imposing stone and turf longhouses found in Orkney and Shetland, with their bow-sides, benches along the walls and a long central hearth. Evidence from excavations at Kilpheder on South Uist, Lephin on Mull and Dunstaffnage near Oban suggests that, prior to the 12th century, Norse settlements in the Hebrides and Argyll coast were composed of small rectangular buildings constructed in turf, timber or wattle, some semi-sunken into the ground. Such buildings leave little trace, particularly if later communities used the same site and built over the Norse settlement.

After Norse control was established, Luing's population paid taxes and tribute and provided labour and resources, perhaps much as they had done in the days of *Dál Riata*. In Ireland the Norse contributed significantly to economic activity through the establishment of trading centres at Dublin and elsewhere. They may have made a different economic impact in the Inner Hebrides and neighbouring mainland. Environmental data from the Oban area show a final phase of woodland clearance prior to the turn of the millennium, the extensive deforestation releasing land for farming as well as providing timber for fuel, building and the construction and repair of boats. Norse fishing communities were doing well, and agriculture was expanding. Other natural resources may also have been of interest. It is claimed that slate was first discovered on Belnahua by Norwegians in the 12th century.

Lords and Kings of the Isles

At the turn of the millennium the Norse had lived in the Hebrides for many generations, and a Gaelic-Norse world had emerged. A powerful dynasty of Gaelic-Norse 'Sea Kings' was established, ruling a huge maritime Kingdom of Man and the Isles. This was a world with international connections. Warriors from the Isles, Kintyre and Argyll fought at the battle of Clontarf in Ireland in 1014, which was won by the Irish High King and ended the power of the Vikings in Ireland. In the early 12th century, during the forty-year reign of Olaf Godredsson, there were links with Orkney, Scotland and England, forged in part through marriage alliances. One alliance was to have profound consequences for Luing's future.

In 1140 Olaf's daughter Ragnhild married Somerled, Lord of Argyll and Kintyre. Little is known about Somerled's origins, but DNA evidence from his descendants show Norse ancestry by the male line. It's possible that Somerled's Norse-Gaelic family came from around the Firth of Lorn. The Orkneyinga Saga, written in the 1220s, describes Somerled's family as the Dalverjar from the Dales on the shores of *Skotlandsfjorðr*, suggested by leading experts to be the Firth of Lorn.

In 1154 a leading magnate in the Kingdom of Man and the Isles, alienated by the tyrannical behaviour of the young king Godred the Black, proposed that Somerled's son Dugald – who had royal blood through his mother Ragnhild – be made King of the Isles. A sea battle off Islay ensued in 1156, leading to a partition of the Isles: Godred kept the Western Isles, Skye and the Isle of Man, but ceded the southern isles, including Mull,

Jura and Islay, to Somerled. A further sea battle in 1158 led to Somerled seizing all of the Kingdom of Man and the Isles, which was confirmed by the King of Norway later that year.

Somerled's control over this vast kingdom, extending from the Irish Sea to the northern tip of the Western Isles, lasted only until 1164, when he died in a battle against the Scottish Kingdom at Renfrew. After this the 1156 partition appears to have been reinstated, Godred regaining his part and Somerled's sons and descendants, the MacSorleys, sharing the Lordship of Argyll and the Isles. Though historical evidence is scarce, Somerled's sudden death led to a period of dynastic struggles and shifting territorial control between Somerled's three sons Ranald, Dugald and Angus. Somerled is thought to have been buried on Iona, where his daughter Bethoc was prioress of the nunnery.

It appears that after Somerled's death Dugald gained Lismore, Coll, Tiree, Mull and north Jura, and possibly their surrounding smaller islands. This might have included Luing, but we cannot be certain and control may have fluctuated. Dugald's descendants became the Clan MacDougall, who, initially at least, were the most powerful of the Lords of the Isles. Ranald gained lands and islands to the south, notably Islay and Kintyre, but was defeated in 1192 by his brother Angus. Angus and his sons were killed in turn by Ranald's sons on Skye in 1210, ending this line of the family and enabling Ranald's son Donald to regain his father's lands. Donald founded the Clan MacDonald, rivals to the MacDougalls.

Kilchattan parish church

It's at this time, at the end of the 12th century, that parish churches began to be built in Argyll, including the church of Kilchattan (24), which served Luing, Shuna, Torsa and neighbouring small islands. The diocese of Argyll, with its cathedral at Lismore, was created by 1189, influenced by Somerled's sons

Ronald and Dugald. While Somerled had been a supporter of the Columban or 'Irish' Church, his sons were influential in introducing a Latinised church and the reformed continental orders (Cistercian, Benedictine, Augustinian, etc.) to Argyll and the Isles. This change established a centralised and hierarchical system of control, both religious and secular in nature.

Kilchattan parish church is a northern outlier of a series of similar churches built by Somerled's son Ronald, mostly in Kintyre which he controlled. A little later in date his brother Dugald established parish churches further north, including on the islands of Mull, Coll, Tiree and Lismore and parts of the mainland. Monasteries also benefited, with new stone buildings on Iona and also on Eileach an Naoimh in the Garvellachs. Lime mortar was introduced in the 12th century, transforming church and secular architecture and allowing more durable and elaborate structures to be built. Earlier structures were built of un-mortared stone and timber, which was in short supply following the major decline in woodland along the western seaboard. Weather may also have been a factor. The Medieval Warm Period increased

Kilchattan old parish church

farming surpluses, and therefore tribute and rent, enabling more to be spent on stone buildings, symbols of power and status.

Divided loyalties

Castles were also important at this time, which was marked by territorial disputes and conflicts. The MacDougalls held several strategic castles including Dunstaffnage and Dunollie and the fortress of Dun Chonnuill in the Garvellachs, visible from Luing and commanding the Firth of Lorn. Military power was essential, especially as Dugald's grandson Ewen was under pressure from both the Scottish and Norwegian Kings to clarify his allegiance. While the islands remained subject to the King of Norway, mainland territories belonged to the King of the Scots.

From the 1220s onwards Scottish Kings took diplomatic and military steps to control the islands. In 1230 a Norwegian expedition to the Isles was partly directed at ensuring the MacDougalls stayed loyal. In 1249 Scottish King Alexander II sailed his fleet of galleys past Luing to negotiate with Ewen MacDougall, Lord of Argyll and King of the Isles, but Alexander fell ill and died on the isle of Kerrera. Ewen's power was weakened, Icelandic Annals suggesting that he may have been temporarily displaced by his cousin Dugald MacRuari, another descendant of Somerled.

A decisive moment came in 1263, when King Haakon IV of Norway arrived with a massive fleet of boats to reassert his control of the islands. Ewen refused to join the Norwegian expedition and had to relinquish his island possessions. Mull, Coll and Tiree were granted by King Haakon to Dugald MacRuari. The expedition was not a success, suffering delays, stormy weather, a disastrous skirmish at Largs and Haakon's death in Orkney on the way home. In 1266 the Treaty of Perth ceded control of the Hebrides to Scotland. Ewen's loyalty to the Scottish crown paid off, the MacDougalls regaining their former lands and Ewen's son Alexander becoming Lord of Argyll.

Boat with sail and animal head prow on south wall of Kilchattan church

Boat graffiti: Scottish or Norwegian?

Several-stones in the southern and northern outer walls of Kilchattan church are inscribed with graffiti, including a significant number of boats (24). One large stone in the southern wall has a particularly important concentration of graffiti, including what appear to be a fleet of boats and two crosses. Two of the Kilchattan boats have animal heads on their prows, while other graffiti appear to show a square sail and a wind-vane.

Experts agree that the graffiti were carved during the 13th century, but do they depict Scottish or Norwegian boats? The Argyll historian Marion Campbell of Kilberry argued that the Kilchattan graffiti may have recorded the passing of King Alexander's fleet on his way to negotiate with Ewen MacDougall, Lord of Argyll and King of the Isles, in 1249. But she also noted a resemblance to a wooden stick from Bergen in Norway carved with a runic inscription and boat graffiti, dated to 1250-1300.

Denis Rixson, an expert on West Highland galleys, suggests that the graffiti may have been carved at the time of King Haakon's great venture of 1263, in the same way as the runes cut in St Molaise's Cell on Holy Isle in Arran. He too notes similarities to

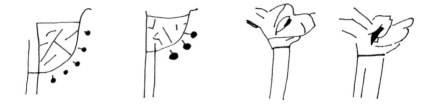

Wind-vanes and animal head prows carved on Bergen stick

Wind-vane and boat with animal head prow carved on Kilchattan church

carvings on the Bergen Stick, including triangular wind vanes on the end-posts of one of the boats, which are known from Viking sources. The Bergen stick is a 25cm long piece of juniper wood, found during excavations at the historic harbour dock in Bergen, Norway's royal centre. A fleet of ships is depicted, some of high status with wind-vanes, animal heads and tall stems, similar to those depicted on the Kilchattan graffiti. King Haakon IV was known for his formidable naval fleet, which may be the subject of the Bergen stick graffiti.

Support for a Norwegian association of the boat graffiti comes too from an expert on Medieval church graffiti, who has suggested that the compass-type cross symbol carved alongside several boats on the south wall might be a type of *vegvisir*, a Norse apotropraic symbol providing protection against rough weather.

Boats and crosses on south wall of Kilchattan church

A Norwegian expert on Medieval boats suggests that the symbol might be a variant of a Christian cross, which would have also been a very powerful protective symbol at this time. Given the difficulties of the journey they might well have sought protection from the elements. King Haakon's fleet may have numbered as many as 120 vessels, and would have included boats from Norway, Orkney and the Hebrides. Its journey, which is described in King Haakon's Saga, included the Sounds of Jura and Luing, making it very possible that use was made of the safe harbours of Luing.

Lordship of the Isles: MacDonalds and MacLeans

The MacDougalls' hold on their vast insular and mainland territory lasted until the end of the 13th century, but their opposition to Robert the Bruce during the Wars of Independence led to their downfall. In 1308-9 Bruce's naval forces sailed past Luing intent on bringing the MacDougalls to heel. A skirmish is said to have taken place on an island in the Sound of Seil and a battle at Kilninver. In 1309, after losing a decisive battle at the Pass of Brander, the MacDougalls were stripped of their lands and titles,

> *At their height the MacDonald Lords of the Isles ruled a vast area from Ross-shire and the Great Glen to Ayrshire, including the Hebrides, Western Isles and Argyll mainland. Islay was their home, and Finlaggan the administrative and symbolic centre of the Lordship. For nearly 200 years, the Lordship was militarily powerful, able to call on loyal clans, vast fleets of galleys and large numbers of professional warriors. Castles were built to defend the Lordship and assert its power. The Lords were important patrons of Gaelic art and culture, including monumental sculpture, music and poetry. The end came in 1493 when King James IV of Scotland seized their estates and titles. It took the crown a further hundred years or more to finally bring the Lords to heel.*

which were divided amongst King Robert I's western supporters, notably the Campbells and the MacDonalds.

Establishing who acquired Luing at this time is difficult, as so few documents have survived. In 1321, Torsa and a neighbouring mainland area were granted to a younger son of the leading Campbell lord Sir Cailean Mor, in exchange for the service of a 24-oar galley, a deal typical of this period when access to galleys and warriors was essential for maintaining power. A lost charter by King Robert I granted Mull and Tiree to the 'King of Argyll' Alexander MacDonald of Islay, and it's probable that Luing was among the lands and islands gained by the MacDonalds at this time. But the deaths of Alexander MacDonald in 1318 and Robert I in 1329 created power vacuums at local and national levels. In 1343 John of Islay, the new leader of the MacDonalds and first Lord of the Isles, received a charter from the new king David II of a huge tract of land and islands, which included Luing.

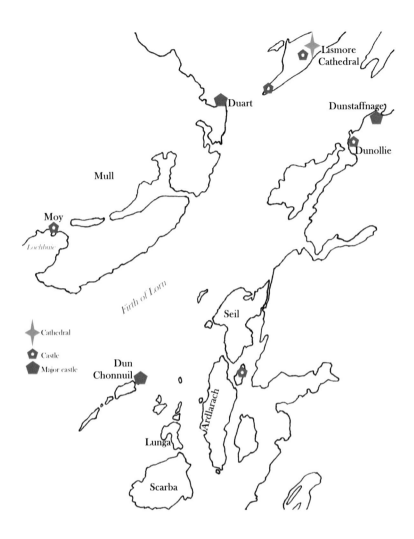

Legend:
- ✦ Cathedral
- ⬠ Castle
- ⬟ Major castle

Map labels: Lismore Cathedral, Duart, Dunstaffnage, Dunollie, Mull, Moy, Lochbuie, Seil, Firth of Lorn, Dun Chonnuil, Ardlarach, Lunga, Scarba

Luing's Late Medieval World

In the 14th century Ardlarach on Luing was granted by the Lord of the Isles to Maclean of Duart along with the sea-girt fortress of Dun Chonnuill. Maclean of Lochbuie was granted lands including Lunga and Scarba. Militarily powerful, the Macleans held castles and lands either side of the strategically important Firth of Lorn, playing a key role in the defence of the Lordship of the Isles. To the north of Luing was Lismore with the Cathedral of the Diocese of Argyll. Luing lay on political and ecclesiastical boundaries, a difficult place to be in Late Medieval times.

With Campbells expanding to the east and MacDougalls laying claim to previously-held territory, Luing may have continued to experience tensions and conflicts over ownership of land. In 1354 an agreement was signed on Seil, which restored to John MacDougall some mainland areas, as well as Coll and part of Tiree, but confirmed John MacDonald's control of other lands and islands.

Luing appears still to have been in MacDonald hands as, in 1390, Donald MacDonald, Lord of the Isles, granted Dun Chonnuill in the Garvellachs and the 'two pence land' of Ardlarach in Luing to Lachlan Maclean of Duart, a grant previously made by Donald's father. This 1390 charter is the earliest reference to a place on Luing. The land of Ardlarach may have served the important island fortress of Dun Chonnuill, providing shelter for galleys and cattle and grain to maintain the Lords' retinue and military forces. Two structures with views of Dun Chonnuill – one on a promontory above Blackmill Bay (36), the other on a ridge at Park further north (45) – might be related to Ardlarach's role at this period. It's not known if the rest of Luing was held directly by the MacDonalds, or was granted to the Macleans or to another clan or supporter.

Lachlan Maclean was one of the four 'greatest of the nobles' on the Lord of the Isles' Council, who played a leading role in the military defence of the Lordship. Another of the four great nobles was Lachlan's brother Hector Maclean of Lochbuie, who also received lands from Donald MacDonald including Kilmory on Scarba and Lunga. The granting of lands either side of the Firth of Lorn and the Sounds of Jura and Luing to two leading nobles, the Maclean brothers, aimed to secure several strategically important sea routes.

Lachlan and Hector were not new to the area, as their father John Dubh had already held Ballachuan on Seil (and probably lands in Duart and Lochbuie on Mull). Together with Luing's safe harbours, they could control the important sheltered sea route from Islay and Kintyre past Luing to Morvern, Lochaber and Glencoe. It seems that Seil was also one of the places where the Lords of the Isles held assemblies and issued charters, enabling inhabitants of Luing to witness – and play a role in – the defence and administration of the Lordship of the Isles for most of the 14th and 15th centuries.

Medieval maritime defence: watch and ward

From the 11th to 15th centuries Luing belonged to Kings and Lords for whom sea power and systems of marine defence were paramount. A system of coastal defence, including promontory forts and beacons, enabled Lords and local populations to monitor sea traffic, protect their own boats and facilitate the ex-action of passage and landing taxes. The good harbours of Luing were well known to mariners; they were mentioned in the sailing instructions, or 'rutter', prepared for an expedition by King James V in 1540 to pacify the Isles, and writing in 1549 Archdeacon Monro described Luing as having *'a havin sufficient for highland galleys in it'*. Sea transport was not only for military purposes or raiding, but also for trade, merchants exporting wool, hides and grain and importing wine and luxury goods. Boats transporting pilgrims to and from Iona and the monastery on Eileach an Naoimh would also have been a common sight.

The use of promontory sites to create a network of 'watch and ward' has been demonstrated in the Isle of Man during Medieval times. A cluster of promontory forts are situated within 10km of Castle Rushen, a major castle on the south coast of the Isle of Man, suggesting they functioned as a network to provide forward intelligence of galley activity off the southwest coast of the island. Seventeenth century Manx records list the places where 'day and night watches' were kept, hills for day watch, hills and ports for night watch. Several sites on Luing overlook important sea lanes

West Ardluing promontory fort overlooking Sound of Luing

or harbours, and could have played a similar role in the defence of the Kingdoms and Lordship of the Isles.

A substantial promontory earthwork on the west side of Ardluing overlooks the Sounds of Jura and Luing (33), while a smaller earthwork sits on a promontory at the southern tip of Ardluing (32), with far-reaching views down the Sound of Jura. On a promontory above Blackmill Bay is an interesting square structure set inside an enclosure (36), with views over a large bay, down the Sound of Luing and north-west to Dun Chonnuill.

At the north end of the island are several sites from where it is possible to observe traffic in the Firth of Lorn and moving through Cuan Sound, including a walled cave (2) and a small hill-top structure (3). On the eastern side of Luing, where several safe harbours are located, there are further sites: an enclosing wall and structure on a promontory above the anchorage south of Cuan (9), and a D-shaped stone enclosure on an islet in Ardluing, protecting a large tidal bay (28). The earthwork of Dùn Ablaich north-east of Ardlarach (41), now in the middle of a bog, might once have watched over galleys laid up over the winter months. Not knowing the dates of these structures, we can only speculate on their function.

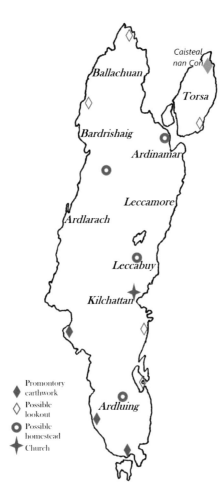

Caisteal nan Con

Ballachuan

Torsa

Bardrishaig

Ardinamar

Leccamore

Ardlarach

Leccabuy

Kilchattan

Ardluing

◆ Promontory earthwork
◇ Possible lookout
◎ Possible homestead
✦ Church

Late Medieval Luing

*By the 13th century a parish church was built at Kilchattan and Luing was
divided into townships. Evidence suggests there may have been townships
with substantial homesteads at Ardinamar, Ardlarach, Leccabuy and
Ardluing. Promontory earthworks and lookouts watched over sea routes and
harbours. By the 16th century there were eight townships, and on Torsa a
castle had been built.*

Religion, rebellion and conflict

By the end of the 15th century, the Lordship of the Isles was collapsing, and in 1493 John MacDonald, Lord of the Isles, forfeited his estates and titles to King James IV of Scotland. In 1500 King James gave control of the Isles to Archibald Campbell, 2nd Earl of Argyll, hoping that this would bring a troublesome region to heel. The deaths of the King and Earl along with many others at the Battle of Flodden in 1513, and the aggressive stance taken towards Scotland by the victor Henry VIII of England, set in train decades of political instability. In the Isles, the rise of the Campbells did not go down well with many leading clans. The 16th century was far from peaceful, bringing difficult – and sometimes dangerous – times for island communities. Religious change from the 1560s compounded the situation, which was not fully resolved until the end of the 17th century.

The Earls of Argyll and Macleans of Duart
In 1513, the new King James V granted the lands of Luing, Torsa and Shuna to Colin, the 3rd Earl of Argyll. Later on, royal grants in the 1540s confirmed the feudal superiority of the Earl of Argyll or his heir to the three islands. But whatever was agreed between the King and Earl did not mean that all was well in the islands, or with clans holding hereditary claims to land.

Land was the main economic resource, providing subsistence for the majority of the population and rent and tribute for clan chiefs, enabling them to maintain their prestige and lifestyle, as well as their galleys and military forces. The introduction of written titles to land sometimes conflicted with hereditary rights – a clan's *dùthchas* – and not all clans benefited. The Earl of Argyll held his lands as a vassal of the crown, but these could be granted to others, in return either for service or a fee (feu). Land became a tool for punishing clan chiefs who fell out of favour because of their rebellious or uncooperative behaviour, or for rewarding others for their support. Changes in the ownership of land were sometimes made by the Earl of Argyll to resolve clan feuds, as happened with Luing.

During the early decades of the 15th century Luing, Torsa and Shuna were held under feu by MacDougalls; but in 1545 the MacDougalls surrendered the islands to the Earl of Argyll, who granted the feu to Hector Mòr Maclean of Duart in exchange for land on the Rinns of Islay, which had become a cause of violent feuding between Macleans and MacDonalds. Hector Mòr Maclean of Duart had just become the Earl's father-in-law, and the grant of lands on Luing, Torsa and Shuna was made "in return for service by land and by sea". Maintaining control in a region occupied by powerful and assertive clans involved a number of stratagems by the Earl of Argyll, including marital alliances, grants of land, bonds of allegiance and military force backed by experienced soldiers, fleets of galleys, castles and artillery.

Territorial feuding between island clans was so bad that in 1540 King James V toured the Hebrides with a naval fleet as a way of asserting royal authority and bringing rebellious clans to heel. He obtained the submission of leading chiefs, including Hector Mòr Maclean of Duart. The 'good harbours' of Luing and Seil may have been used by his fleet, as they were mentioned in the 'rutter' – a set of sailing instructions – prepared by King James's pilot, Alexander Lindsay, for the 1540 expedition.

Luing, Torsa and Shuna were inherited by Hector Mòr's son Hector Og, who in 1573 granted six merklands on Luing to his 'beloved spouse' Lady Janet Campbell, half-sister of the 5th Earl of Argyll. This property on Luing was described as having a 'place', that is a house of some substance. The only township on Luing known to have been valued at six merklands is Kilchattan, so this may have been the property given to Lady Campbell. With its church and rich arable, it was an appropriate property to grant to someone important. Hector Og died soon afterwards, succeeded in 1574 by Lachlan Mòr, who was Chief of the Macleans until his death in 1598 at a battle on Islay with the MacDonalds, their bloody feud having continued. As was normal at this period Lachlan had been fostered as a child, his foster-father being Hector Allansoun Maclean, described in a 1574 Bond of Manrent as 'Hector Maclean of Ardluing'. Similar bonds of loyalty and maintenance had been made by the preceding Earls of Argyll to Hector Allansoun's father. His status in clan Maclean suggests that Ardluing may also have been a property of some importance.

Clan Maclean was powerful militarily, commanding fleets of galleys and substantial numbers of professional soldiers who could fight for clan interests and be hired as mercenaries to Irish lords. As Clan Chief, Lachlan Mòr pursued his interests ruthlessly, engaging in frequent raids and feuds with other Macleans, Campbells and MacDonalds, and breaking traditional alliances and laws. But the Earl of Argyll was also ruthless in deploying his might against recalcitrant clan leaders. Lachlan Mòr had chosen not to marry a Campbell and was in trouble financially, owing rent for lands he held in feu. Luing was twice attacked under orders of Colin Campbell, the 6th Earl of Argyll, the second in deliberate defiance of the Privy Council, to which Lachlan Mòr had submitted formal complaints. In December 1577, Dugald Campbell of Inverawe landed on Luing with 200 armed troops and seized 500 cattle, 200 horses and 1200 sheep. They also seized the clothes from women and children and took three men prisoners. Luing was attacked again in January 1579. This time they killed one man and his servant, and laid 'violent hands' on George Smollett, Maclean's Captain on the island, who was severely wounded and held to ransom.

In 1579/80 Lachlan Mòr sold Torsa and twelve merklands on Luing to Duncan MacDougall of Dunollie. In 1580 he sold a further four merklands of Luing to Archibald Campbell of Melfort, and in 1583 he gave Colin Campbell of Lundie, the Earl of Argyll's second son, the sasine (title of legal possession) of the four merks land of Ballachuan as security for a debt, which, if he failed to pay, would grant Lundie a charter of the annual rent from Luing. Continued feuding between Macleans and MacDonalds led to Lachlan Mòr's imprisonment – along with two leading MacDonalds – in Edinburgh in 1590. Though not dispossessed of their property, they were each fined an enormous sum. The price paid to Campbell of Ardkinglas for Lachlan Mòr's release in 1591 was the Isle of Luing. After Lachlan Mòr's violent death in 1598, his son Hector Og became Chief of Clan Maclean.

The Earls of Argyll and Breadalbane
If the people of Luing had hopes for more peaceful times during the 17th century these were soon dashed by continued clan disputes and serious religious and political conflicts, which had significant consequences on the landholding of Luing. In 1603, Colin Campbell of Lundy, a son of the 6th Earl of Argyll, made a claim against Maclean of Duart and Campbell of Ardkinglas for non-payment of the yearly rent of £500 for the lands of Luing, which he then acquired for £8,000. This was followed by a warning to the inhabitants to move, possibly in order to give tenancies to his family and supporters or to raise rents. Luing then seems to have been passed by the 7th Earl of Argyll to one of his daughters as part of her dowry, but in 1614 the 7th Earl's indebtedness led to him redeeming her dowry lands for £9 Scots. In 1619 the 7th Earl renounced Protestantism in favour of the

Catholic religion of his second wife, and surrendered his estates to his son Archibald, who became the 8th Earl of Argyll in 1638.

The proprietary interests of the Campbells were pursued ruthlessly by Archibald the 8th Earl of Argyll. In 1629 and 1630 the lands of Kilchattan, Leccabuy and Ardluing, as well as the '*stewardry, coronership, and sheriffdom of the lands and isles of Loyng, Torsay, Shuna and others*' were resigned to him by the feuars, who had been local Campbells. He quickly moved to assert control. During 1630-31 several attempts were made to evict tenants. Tenants often resisted and refused to move, including on Luing. In 1634 another attempt was made to evict the sitting tenants on Luing, Torsa and Shuna. The aim may have been to replace existing tenants with Archibald's followers or to raise rents, or both. When the 8th Earl, a Presbyterian, committed Clan Campbell to the Covenanting Movement in 1638, many clans in the region joined the opposing Royalist cause because of their treatment by the Campbells.

The 8th Earl of Argyll was a leading Covenanter, but, after early military and political successes, ended up ruined and

Covenanters were 17th century supporters of the Presbyterian Church of Scotland, who opposed King Charles I of England over church structure and doctrine. In particular, Presbyterians rejected government by bishops (which was supported by Episcopalians) and opposed royal interference in church affairs. In 1638 thousands of Scots signed the National Covenant, and after winning victories in 1639 and 1640 took control of Scotland. A period of defeats and successes followed, but after the 1688 Glorious Revolution the Church of Scotland was re-established as wholly Presbyterian.

deeply in debt in 1654. After the Restoration of the Monarchy, he was beheaded for treason in 1661, and his estates forfeited. The title of Earl was restored in 1663 along with the estate, but it was still heavily in debt. In 1669 a 'warning to leave' was issued to tenants on Luing and Torsa, not it seems with the intention of evicting them but as an attempt to renegotiate the terms of their tenancies and introduce a cash component to help pay debts. From rental documents, there is little change in the names of tenants on Luing and Torsa at this time, so it seems that most stayed in place, though the attempt to extract cash rents from them seems not to have worked.

The 9th Earl fared little better than his father. His rebellion in 1685 against King James II and VII led to him too being beheaded. In 1654 the Netherlorn estate, including Luing, had been given in feu to Lord Neil Campbell of Ardmaddy, a younger brother of the 9th Earl. The Macleans of Duart formally contin-ued as feuars of Luing until 1674, but by then they were sub-stantially in debt to the Earls of Argyll. Following several years of legal proceedings and military expeditions against the Macleans, in 1678 a fleet of galleys, birlinns and boats organised by the Earl of Argyll landed on Mull and took possession of Maclean's cattle, castle and other parts of his estate. The Campbells finally had full access to Maclean's lands and the rents they generated.

After Lord Neil Campbell's death in 1692, Luing and Nether-lorn were sold to John Campbell, the 1st Earl of Breadalbane, a Royalist and supporter of the Restoration of the monarchy. Called 'Slippery John' by some, he was known for his ambition and political manoeuvring. Luing and Netherlorn remained part of the Earl of Breadalbane's vast estate for the next 230 years. The change of owner occurred at a time of hardship and disruption; the last decade of the 17th century was a time of foreign wars, economic troubles, poor weather and famine, as well as religious repression and brutal clan conflict. Penal laws against Catholics were reimposed in 1689, and in 1692 there was the infamous massacre of MacDonalds at Glencoe by Campbells. The political situation was volatile and there were new taxes to pay, to raise money for the army and navy.

Religious and clan conflict

Luing's inhabitants were affected by the religious and political conflicts. Prior to the adoption of Protestantism by the Scottish Reformation Parliament in 1560, the official religion had been Catholic. In 1592 a full Presbyterian system was adopted, but it took another hundred years to settle the nature of the reformed Scottish Church. The 17th century was marked by conflict between Presbyterianism (as supported by the Covenanters) and Episcopacy, while Catholicism survived in parts of the region, albeit illegally. Combined with clan conflicts, considerable damage was done to the local economy and population.

Luing was probably affected by the 'ravaging' of Argyll in 1644 and 1646/7, when the Covenanter forces supported by the Campbells sought to defeat the Royalists led by Alasdair MacColla (otherwise known as Sir Alexander MacDonald), whose aim was to regain clan MacDonald lands. The raids, counter-raids and retribution affected crops and brought famine and hardship, from which the region took years to recover. Mac-Colla had his supporters on Luing, notably the poet Dorothy Brown (*Diorbhail Nic a' Bhriuthainn)* who wrote a love poem to Alasdair after apparently seeing his ships pass through the Sound of Luing in their campaign against the Campbells. Gaelic Scotland produced a number of distinguished female poets, some of whom were professional bardic poets. Dorothy's poetry and songs imply a level of education and literary skill, as well as familiarity with different poetic traditions. Dorothy was buried in Kilchattan churchyard, though sadly there is no headstone to mark her burial place.

The return of the Monarchy in 1660 and Restoration of the Episcopacy led to prolonged conflict between Presbyterians and the Bishops of the Episcopalian establishment. Church ministers had to accept the new situation or lose their livings. Up to a third of the ministry refused, and some took to preaching in open fields in conventicles. The Scottish Privy Council attempted to end the dissent by 'Indulging' ministers, allowing them to return to their churches on condition that they stayed silent on the issues dividing the Church. The last Minister at Kilchattan was John Duncanson, who was 'indulged' in 1670 and allowed to preach in Kilchattan parish, along with Alexander MacLean, another 'outed' minister. In 1685 John Duncanson was involved in Argyll's Rising, the attempt to overthrow the Catholic King James II and VII led by the 9th Earl of Argyll. The Rising was unsuccessful, and troops loyal to King James swept through Argyll committing 'cruel ravages on the estates and tenantry' of the Earl of Argyll. The Earl was executed, while other supporters were punished by being sent to the colonies, stripped of their wealth or imprisoned. John Duncanson was imprisoned at Campbeltown, where he died in 1687.

Only in 1690 was the reformed Scottish Church finally settled as Presbyterian. By this time Kilchattan church appears to have been abandoned as a place of worship, although it continued as

Old Graves at Kilchattan

a place of burial (24). The earliest dated gravestone inside the church is 1680. Kilchattan was joined with Kilbrandon on Seil to form a united parish, and in 1735 a new parish church was built at North Cuan on Seil.

Landlords and tenants: townships and farming

Seventeenth century estate documents provide the first documented evidence of some of the people who lived on Luing, the rent they paid and how they farmed the land. Luing had three mills, showing the importance of grain. Later on, cattle became more important. The island was divided into 'towns', each with several tenant families, jointly responsible for farming the land and paying rent. Major changes took place in the late 17th century and then more substantially in the 18th century, as the landowner sought to 'Improve' his estate and generate more income.

The old 'towns'

By the end of the 16th century Luing was divided into nine or ten 'towns' (fermtouns in Scots), with Torsa as another town. These were not towns in the modern sense, but defined areas of land, each containing a mix of arable and pasture and access to water and other resources such as peat for fuel. Each town had a fixed value, on the basis of which rent was calculated. The tenants in each town were jointly responsible for paying the rent, which until the late 17th century was paid in grain (oatmeal and bere), other farm products and labour services.

The division of Luing into towns, for purposes of valuation and establishing the rent due, had by then been in place for many centuries. A land-based system of assessment may have first developed in association with the transition from the kin-based society of *Dál Riata* to the Norse-Gaelic lordships of the 10th and 11th centuries. The Norse imposed tax (*skat*) on land they controlled, and there was a system of rents and services in the Hebrides and Kintyre from the time of the formal agreement in 1098 AD between the Scots King Edgar and Norwegian King Magnus to the ceding of control by Norway in the 1266 Treaty of Perth. The latter Treaty ceded to Scotland rights in the Hebrides to 'homages and rents, services and all their rights and pertinents within their borders'.

Evidence suggests that the emergence of the Gaelic-Norse Kingdoms of the Isles was a pivotal point in the way that land was used, occupied and assessed. Instead of renders and obligations to a chief being burdened on the group or family, the amount of land occupied became the basis for establishing the obligations, renders and services due to the lord. Analysis of environmental data in the Oban area has shown rapid and permanent deforestation from around 1000 AD, possibly linked to the development of a distinctive land-use strategy and settlement pattern, perhaps part and parcel of this new land-based system of tax and control. A variety of units of valuation were in use in Medieval Scotland: ploughgates, pennylands, davachs and, on Luing, merklands. The regularity of town values across mid-Argyll and Knapdale – typically four merklands per town – suggests a planned system of land units, originating perhaps at the time of Somerled's sons in the late 12th century AD, when the parochial and diocesan structure was also established. The Kings and Lords of the Isles were not only great warriors and sailors, but also highly-organised administrators, planners and law-makers.

The number of towns on Luing may have grown over time. Elsewhere in the region the numbers of towns increased significantly between the 14th and 18th centuries: in Morvern, the number increased from seven in the 14th century to twenty in the late 15th and fifty-three in the mid-18th, with comparable increases in

Islay and North Uist. If a similar process occurred on Luing this might suggest three or four towns in the 14th century, compared to nine or ten in the 17th century. Three sites on Luing could be substantial structures dating to the later Medieval period, perhaps indicating the location of the early towns: a substantial circular stone structure on a promontory above the shore at Ardinamar (13); a circular stone-and-turf structure on a promontory south-west of Park (45); and a circular mound with revetment and access track at Leccabuy (20) close to the Medieval church at Kilchattan (24). Structures at the 'Old Town' of Ardluing might suggest a fourth Medieval town (30).

Most towns on Luing were four merklands in value: Nether Ardlarach (40), Over Ardlarach (42), Ardinamar (13), Bardrishaig (8) and Ballachuan (5), with Torsa also valued at four merklands. Ardluing was eight merklands, but may have been farmed as two towns (30). Kilchattan, which contained extensive arable land and the church, was six merklands (25). In the 17th and 18th centuries Leccabuy was five merklands (20), and Leccamore varied between three and four merklands (18). The valuations remained remarkably similar over time. A 1596 report on the military capacity of the Isles indicates the extent of Luing at 40 merklands, identical to that a hundred years later.

The valuation of towns in the Highlands and Islands was based on their arable, not on the total land area or its overall productive capacity. Access to other resources, such as pasture, were append-aged rights, proportional to the possession of assessed arable. Even so, it appears that each town possessed a similar range of resources (arable land, grazing, woodland, peat bogs and access to fishing), able to sustain a group of people throughout the year.

Dykes and enclosures

Visitors to Medieval Luing in mid-summer would have seen fields of growing oats and barley, cattle, sheep and horses grazing on

the pasture land and scattered
settlements of small turf-walled
houses and farm buildings with
small turf enclosures. The landscape was, however, devoid of the
network of banks, dykes and walls
visible today. An open field system
prevailed for much of the Medieval period in the West Highlands
and Islands. Physical boundaries
between towns (march dykes) and
between arable and pasture (head
dykes) were perhaps not built
until the 17th and 18th centuries.
Instead, the location of boundaries
would have been marked by big
stones and sometimes heaps of
ashes, as well as by natural features
such as watercourses and water-

Turf-and-stone march dyke between
Ballachuan and Bardrishaig

sheds ('as wind and water shear'), or, as sometimes seems to be
the case on Luing, the prominent edge of an escarpment.

The earliest historical record mentioning boundaries on Luing
dates to the 17th century. Around 1660 court acts for Netherlorn
and its islands opened with an order to tenants '*to mak sufficient
merch dykes*' of '*diviot, earth and steane*' and to have a '*poindfauld*',
an enclosure to which animals found destroying corn or grass
were to be taken. If grain or grass was destroyed, compensation
had to be paid by the owner of the offending animal, and fines
were imposed on tenants if they failed to build or maintain the
dykes. The open fields meant that crops of oats and barley had
to be protected from farm animals during the growing season.
Head dykes around the permanently-cultivated arable areas were
the solution in some areas and on larger islands. In other areas,

where the arable land of neighbouring towns lay close together, march dykes were built along the town boundaries. It is likely that most of the circuitous turf-and-stone dykes still visible on Luing were constructed at this time, quite possibly following the line of earlier boundaries.

Farming the land

Luing had long been renowned for its grain and cattle. In the 16th century it was described as being 'good for corn' and, along with Seil and Shuna, as 'quite rich in cattle and crops'.

The main crops were oats and to a lesser extent bere barley, which was malted and used for brewing ale. Until the introduction of cash rents, tenants paid a large part of their rent in grain. It was also important to landlords wanting to maximise revenue from their estates, as shown by the detailed mid-17th century bye-laws affecting township farming on Seil and Luing, which were among the most advanced in the Western Isles. Bye-laws dealt not only with the management of arable (the wintertoun or infield) but also pasture land (outfield). The bye-laws instructed tenants to divide the town's arable between them equally each year, and to manure their own share of the arable. Crop rotation was undertaken, and, unusually for the Isles, the bye-laws for Luing and Seil required one third of the arable of every town to be left fallow each year. Manuring of arable ground was essential, using animal dung and seaweed.

Unlike many other areas, Luing regularly produced an export-able surplus of grain, even during times of great scarcity such as the famine year of 1696. Black cattle, sheep and horses were also kept, in substantial numbers if the reports of the 'invasions' of 1577 and 1579 are correct. As the pressure grew for rent to be paid in cash, cattle took on more importance.

Pasture land seems also to have been divided annually among the tenants, as there was a provision for tenants to be recompensed for damage done to their grass as well as their corn by their neighbours' animals. As demand for arable grew, suitable areas of the outfield would be cultivated in rotation with periods under pasture. Cultivation of outfield areas was preceded by gathering animals in temporary folds or pens during the summer months ('tathing'), to manure the area scheduled for cultivation the following spring.

Although transhumance was practised, hill pasture was more limited than on other islands and in some cases people and animals moved to small offshore islands during the growing season. Others moved to small settlements – shielings – on hill pasture. The foundations of three roughly-built huts lie close together on a ridge to the west of Leccamore; nearby is a winding old track leading from the pasture grounds down to the farm and the arable fields (16). An unusual cellular structure – with a central stone circle and three attached cells – is located near to the shielings. This might have been used as a lambing pen or animal fold, or perhaps as a dairy for the production of butter and cheese, although a prehistoric origin may also be possible.

Cattle were lucrative, but the relatively limited pasture ground and amount of winter fodder constrained the numbers of animals that could be kept. Bye-laws on 'souming' set limits to the number of animals of each kind allowed on a particular area of land. One of the bye-laws allowed tenants, where they obtained the consent of their landlord, to keep a soum of five goats in place of one cow. Horses were kept as the main beasts of burden.

As part of their rights over the use of town resources, tenants were allowed to cut peat for fuel, and turf and heather for dyke-building, thatching, rope-making and other purposes. Stocks of peat were limited, and bye-laws controlled how the peat was cut, with tenants fined for not conforming to the rules. A court record from 1680 shows that the tenants of Over and Nether Ardlarach and Leccabuy were all fined for cutting their peat wrongly. As wood was in very short supply, the bye-laws stipulated the planting of trees, though court records of 1680 suggest this was widely ignored (insecurity gave tenants little incentive to invest long-term in farm improvement). On the other hand, the requirement to keep a kailyard appears to have been universally respected. Brewing was also regulated, including the quality of the ale, which was sold in brewhouses located at ferry-crossings. Fines were imposed *'for brewing evill drink'*, tasters appointed to regularly check its quality.

As the population increased during the 18th century, there were growing pressures on resources and tensions between subsistence cropping and stock production. Farming had become a struggle to produce enough for the growing population, and by the end of the 18th century high local populations made it essential for those farming the land to maximise subsistence over the generation of cash income.

Grain milling and mills

The importance of grain to the island economy is shown by the presence of three mills on Luing from at least the 17th century to the 19th century, as well as a large number of corn-drying kilns and, later on, gin gangs for threshing attached to farm barns. For many centuries, grain was threshed by hand and milled using a rotary quern, which required a heavy investment of labour, generally by women. In Medieval times landlords tried to forbid their use in homes, so that tenants had to take their grain to the local mill to be ground. In 1284 an Act of the Scottish Parliament limited the use of hand mills to periods of drought or where water was scarce. Nevertheless, they were in use in some areas until the modern period. A quern stone made from garnet-mica schist lies in a garden at Toberonochy, the stone imported from elsewhere in Scotland (or perhaps from Norway and Medieval in date). More common on Luing and Torsa are knocking stones, which

Knocking stone at Cullipool

are large stone mortars used for removing the barley husk; there are examples at Cullipool and beside some of the old farmhouses on Luing and Torsa.

The introduction of mills not only freed up women's labour for other work such as farming and weaving, but generated income for landlords. Simple horizontal mills may have been introduced in early Medieval times. By the 12th century horizontal mills were being built in large numbers across Scotland. The water wheel sits beneath the millstones and turns the upper stone directly, without intermediate gearing. Each township may once have had its own small mill, located on a fast-running burn. It's possible that Blackmill Bay is named after the mill there, as horizontal mills were sometimes called 'black' mills (39).

By the 17th century, mills were part of a strategy by landowners to extract more rent from their lands. Tenants were bound by the terms of their leases to grind their grain at a designated mill (an obligation known as *thirlage*) and to pay the miller a "multure", a proportion of their grain, to do so. Landowners owned the mills, and leased the mills at high rents. Some of the labour services tenants had to provide as part of their lease included maintenance of the mill, lade and dam.

Records from 1710 and 1711 state that *'the three mills of Luing (were) set to Dugald Campbell, paying annually of grassmeal and multure meal £5.6.8., 24 bolls meal'.* Meal was oatmeal, grassmeal

19th century overshot mill at Achafolla (LHG Archives)

was payment for pasturage, and multure meal was the payment by a tenant for having their grain ground there. Documents from 1735 mention three mills on Luing and the annual rent paid by each to the Earl of Breadalbane: at Ardinamir the mill paid over £66 in rent, and at Nether Ardlarach and Leccabuy the mills each paid 10 bolls of grain and over £69. At Ardinamar it's possible there was an earlier horizontal mill upstream from the later overshot mill (13). The Leccabuy mill was probably on the site of the later Achafolla mill (21). The Nether Ardlarach mill may have been at Blackmill Bay (39), where stone foundations and a broken millstone can still be seen.

From around 1750 larger, more efficient vertical mills were built. Water wheels set vertically were turned by water running over (overshot) or under (undershot) them, driving the millstones using intermediate gearing. An overshot mill was built at Ardi-namar, the fragmentary remains of the dam, sluice, lade and mill building still visible alongside the burn (13). Two corn drying kilns and associated buildings suggest that, for a time, this was an important grain processing complex. By 1796 the mill was described as '*quite ruinous*' and generating little return for the miller (and little rent for Breadalbane), due apparently to the farms thirled to the mill failing to pay the victual rent due. The 'Black Miln' was in *'tolerable repair'* and continued in use into the early 19th century, despite a decline in grain production. The mill at Achafolla became the principal mill on the island, a fine overshot mill being constructed in the 19th century; the mill building can still be seen, along with the mill lade, wheel and mill stones (21).

Farm settlements and houses

Towards the end of the 18th century most people on Luing were living in small nucleated settlements, with a cluster of houses and buildings at the heart of each farming township, and in small villages that were developing beside slate quarries at Cullipool (6), Balure (19) and Blackmill Bay (37). Nucleated rural settlements (*bailtean*) were typical across the West Highlands and Islands at this time, though they may not have been characteristic of earlier periods. The *baile* was an amorphous collection of dwellings and barns, often associated with small enclosures, along with occasional mills and other buildings. There was probably also some dispersed settlement, occupied permanently or seasonally.

Evidence of dispersed settlement has been found by the archaeological survey, including a significant number of small isolated houses, some associated with patches of cultivation or small enclosures. More ephemeral evidence, such as platforms cut into the sheltered side of a knoll or sub-rectangular arrangements of stones set in the ground, may be all that remains of the houses of cottars and their families. Many of Luing's inhabitants had no formal tenancy, but occupied a house or tiny plot of land in exchange for labour. Some of these houses may date to the eighteenth century when Luing's population expanded rapidly and pressure on land was intense, while others may be earlier in date.

Prior to the late 18th century, houses and farm buildings of the tenantry were constructed of perishable raw materials

Pre-improvement house at Ardinamar

(wattle, turf and earth), sometimes on dry-stone foundations. The roofs were probably of thatch, supported on wooden cruck trusses, which would have been valuable given the limited supply of timber. At Ardinamar are the remains of a sub-rectangular turf building built on stone foundations with an associated enclosure (13), which may be the only surviving evidence of the pre-Improvement settlement. A hearth would have been located centrally, accompanied by one or more turf benches for sleeping, working or sitting. Turf offered much better insulation than stone or timber alone, and was readily available for construction or repair. The other important pre-Improvement farm building was the threshing barn, with two opposing entrances and oriented to catch the prevailing wind. The stone foundations of a possible early threshing barn are located in a windy position on Achadh dà Chaluim west of Ardinamar (10).

The appearance of Luing's farming settlements and buildings was to change dramatically when the Earl of Breadalbane set about reorganising the Netherlorn estate and its farms in the name of 'Improvement'.

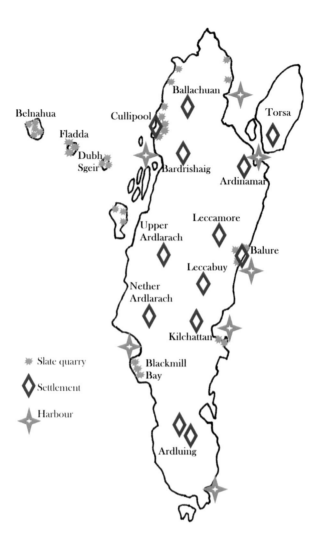

Luing in 1787

In the 1780s, as Improvement took hold, Luing was a busy place. Slate was being quarried around its shores and on offshore islands. Ten settlements were the focus of farming and craft activities, and three grain mills were in operation. Harbours enabled slate and livestock to be exported and goods brought in, and provided a safe refuge during stormy weather.

Improvement and Industry: Transforming the island

The Earls of Breadalbane, like the Earls of Argyll, were 'improving' landlords from early on, keen to extract as much revenue as possible from their estates through land and agricultural reform and by means of extractive industries such as slate quarrying. Efforts to generate more revenue through rent increases, better farm management and commercial quarrying had already started in the 17th century. In the 18th and 19th centuries farming and industry on Luing were transformed.

Rent increases and farm reorganisation
In 1730 tenants in Netherlorn had already been faced with rent increases and the introduction of competitive bidding for tenancies, causing considerable insecurity amongst the tacksmen, tenants and subtenants on Breadalbane's estate. A few years later the Earl tried to sell his lands in Netherlorn, with the exception of Luing and a farm on Kerrera, but this fell through. The priority for Breadalbane, and the factors who managed his estates, was – above all else – maximisation of rental income. In the 1780s surveys and reports were prepared with the aim of 'Dividing Enclosing and otherwise improving' the Netherlorn estate, influenced by economic and social theories of the day.

The 'Improvement' model envisaged a mixed market economy, with wage-labourers living in new settlements and providing labour to resource extraction industries alongside farmers practising commercialised agriculture. As well as slate quarrying, generating more income from the estate was sought by increasing farm production and rents, issuing leases for activities such as milling, commercial fishing, ferries and change houses (inns), and to some extent through military recruitment.

The plans for improving the estate were justified by social improvements for the tenants as well as increased rent for the landowner, as a report of 1794 by the Earl of Breadalbane's Chamberlain for Netherlorn makes clear: *If this plan is adopted, the Reporter thinks (with some confidence) that it may excite a spirit of industry and improvement hitherto unknown amongst these people. The tenants having Leases for such a time will encourage them to bestow their labour and money if they have any in improvements, because they are sure they, or their heirs, will reap the benefits and at the same the Proprietor will have a fair and safe Rent for his Lands and have the satisfaction of seeing his Estate gradually improved.*

The tenants had no say in the matter and from the mid-1780s Luing's multiple-tenant towns were divided into separate farms and crofts, each with one tenant. Runrig was abandoned, and enclosures and subdivisions *"wt stone fences"* – i.e. dry-stone walls – were built. There were strict rules governing how the estate, and the farms and crofts, should be run. The 1787 "Scheme of Regulations and Improvement" included specifications on the farm divisions, systems of rotation, grass management, the building and maintenance of enclosures, management of animals, tree planting, growing of vegetable crops, and much more.

The construction of march dykes was also required from the 1780s onwards as Improvement took hold, with 'proposals for Dividing Enclosing and other ways Improving' farms on the Netherlorn estate featuring in Reports to the Earl of Breadalbane. Payment was made, for example, in 1781/2 for 'a march dyke between Leckamore and Ardinamar'. The previously sinuous march dykes were required to be straightened, and the 'lines of

Division' between the new farms (now 'two merk-lands or half plows' in value) generally built with stone.

The new divisions did not work entirely. A re-survey of the Netherlorn estate around 1798 found that some of the holdings had slipped back into 'run-ridge touns', albeit based around a smaller number of tenants per holding. Further changes were made to the division of Luing into farms and crofts. To assist in the improvement of agriculture, the Earl started a system of incentives – called 'premiums' – for tenants who showed superior industry and skill in farming. Significant investments were made in drainage, reclamation of waste land and new methods of cultivation.

Stone march dyke

New farms and crofts

The new farms reflected the philosophy of 'Improvement', which aimed to bring order and control to a system that was seen as archaic and inefficient. It was out with the old and in with the new. In a letter to the Earl of Breadalbane in 1794, a tenant at Leccabuy noted that he had been obliged to demolish the old buildings and build new ones together with 'an excellent dwelling house' all at his own expense. Tenants were clearly obliged to follow a common plan for the new farmsteads, which had linear ranges of rectangular stone buildings at their core. Some of the linear buildings had three compartments, providing a house, barn and byre. Some had two, either a house with barn or a house with byre. Most had enclosures and a kailyard close by, and away from the farmstead was at least one corn-drying kiln. In the late 18th century, the focus was on grain and cattle, the latter seen by Breadalbane as offering a greater chance of generating more profit and increased rents. More research on Luing's late-18th century farms may shed light on differences in farming practice, and the balance between cattle and grain.

Land was also carved out of the newly reorganised farms to create crofts, some for soldiers returning from the Revolutionary Wars. Two were given in the 1790s to ex-soldiers of the Breadalbane Fencibles, one of these at Ardinamar (12).

Although the suggested division of Luing into single-tenant farms had proved impossible to achieve, the actual division into farms and crofts brought in higher rent. Rents had been increased by over a fifth at the end of the 18th century, and were increased again in 1805, commonly doubling in amount. The significantly

Three battalions of Breadalbane Fencibles were raised by the Earl of Breadalbane to fight for Great Britain in the French revolutionary wars from 1792 to 1799 and in the Irish rebellion from 1795 to 1802. 2,300 men joined in total, 1,600 of whom were from Breadalbane's own estates in Perthshire and Argyll. Promises of land were made to recruits and favours offered to relatives. Tenant families who offered a son felt confident of keeping their lease, while those without a son or who were reluctant to let them go were made to find a substitute, or risk losing their land. Not all returning soldiers received a croft, and petitions to the Earl reveal a great deal of ill-feeling when promises of tenancies or land were not respected.

higher rents combined with poor harvests inevitably led some farm and croft tenants to fall into arrears during the early decades of the 19th century, ultimately losing their tenancies.

The era of the French revolutionary wars, from 1790 to 1815, was one of prosperity and economic growth in the Highlands and Islands. High prices for cattle, kelp, fisheries and weaving brought money into local communities. In 1778 estate records note that 27 tons of kelp, manufactured on the shores of Netherlorn, were sold for £40 10 shillings. The expense of manufacturing is recorded as a mere £3 10 shillings. This period of relative prosperity came to an end around 1815. Bad weather and a period of poor harvests in the 1820s and 1830s added to the economic difficulties. Poor tenant farmers and crofters were especially affected by the declining economic conditions. Although the Netherlorn estate was still exploiting kelp in the early 19th century, records from 1837 and 1838 suggest that it was no longer a profitable activity. The potato famine of 1846 and later years brought considerable hardship, leading to the provision of poor relief and investment in drainage and the construction of dykes and walls, which provided employment. Between 1841 and 1851 Luing's population dropped from 860 to 678, a reflection of the hard times.

The model farm

Further re-organisation and consolidation of holdings took place in the 1850s following a detailed survey of the Netherlorn estate in 1847. Farmsteads built at this time were arranged around a courtyard, each with a stone-built farmhouse and separate byre and barn. Barns had attached horse-gin platforms, enabling horse power to be used to drive threshing machines inside the barn. Examples are the farmsteads of Ballycastle (12) and Park (42).

The biggest change was the building in 1853 of a substantial 'model farm' at Kilchattan (26). At the forefront of agricultural developments, the farm was primarily for raising crops and fattening

19th century farmstead at Ballycastle (LHG Archives)

stock and involved a huge investment. In June 1853, twenty-three masons were employed to construct the new buildings, along with stone quarriers and labourers. A large byre, barn and stables, as well as other smaller buildings, were built. There were even two toilets provided for farm staff. The byre was the second largest in Scotland, and could accommodate nearly 200 cattle. Local whinstone and slate were used for the walls, the best Caithness sandstone for stalls, troughs and paving.

From October to May the cattle were housed inside the byre. During the calving season the nightshift was taken by the farmworkers' wives, who were provided with a small room in the byre. A water tank south of the farm provided drinking water for the cattle, each animal having its own drinking and feeding trough. The waste slurry from the byre was collected in a large underground tank in front of the byre. From this tank it was pumped by steam engine through long cast iron pipes onto the surrounding fields. In the loft above the barn, corn sheaves were stored for threshing.

The model farm caused major disruption to people living at Kilchattan and Ardluing, where farms and crofts were cleared of their tenants. In a letter of July 1853, a critic of Breadalbane publicly admonished him for evicting tenants on his estates, including Luing *'where some twenty-five families lived at the beginning of this year, but who are now cleared off to make room for one tenant, for whom an extensive steading is now being erected'*. It is not known what happened to the families, but some may have moved to Toberonochy and been employed on the model farm. Others left the island entirely; Luing's population dropped from 678 in 1851 to 519 in 1861. Some may have emigrated. In 1853 many people from the Highlands and Islands left on boats destined for Australia and New Zealand.

The mid-19th century was the high point of investment by the Earls of Breadalbane in farming on Luing. From 1782, when the 4th Earl inherited the estate, to the death of the 5th Earl in 1862, the nature and organisation of farming on Luing had been transformed, as were the lives of farming families. But the 5th Earl died childless and the estate passed to a distant cousin, after whose death in 1871 it passed to his son Sir Gavin Campbell, who amassed not only a large number of titles but also debts due to an extravagant lifestyle, bad management and gambling. He died childless in 1922 and his vast estate was sold.

Slate quarrying

The black carbonaceous slate of Argyll's 'slate islands', with its characteristic iron pyrites crystals ('fool's gold'), has been exploited for centuries. An early report mentions a cargo of slates being sent to St Andrews in 1168, and Glasgow Cathedral, founded in 1197, is said to be roofed with it. The first written reference to slate occurs in an account of Netherlorn in 1554, with particular

Clyde puffer passing Belnahua slate island, medieval fortress of Dun Chonnuill behind

mention of Belnahua, whose slate is said to have been discovered by Norwegians in the 12th century. Castle Stalker at Appin, which was built in 1631, was roofed with Easdale slate, and in 1697 Ardmaddy Castle, the home of the Netherlorn estate factor, was re-roofed with local slate. At this time slate was collected from the shores and quarried from the surface by local farm labourers, but an increase in demand for slate and building stone from the end of the 17th century required a more organised and commercial approach.

Initially the quarries were managed by Colin Campbell of Carwhin, the Netherlorn estate factor, with permanent workers and improved methods of quarrying and cutting the slate. In 1745, after the end of the Jacobite Rising, the Earl of Breadalbane instructed Carwhin to establish the Marble and Slate Company of Netherlorn, which took over the existing assets of 600,000 roofing slates and seven sets of quarrying tools for the sum of £826. At this time there were eight crews of four men employed on Easdale, with an annual production of about one million slates per year, mostly for roofing.

In 1751 production started at Cullipool (6) and at Ellenabeich on Seil, and a few years later at Blackmill Bay (37). Kilchattan quarry started in 1766; when the quarry workers' village was established it was given the name of Toberonochy (27). More quarries opened in 1770. A 1787 map shows a quarry settlement at Balure (19). A report of 1805 on the Improvement of farming on the Netherlorn estate also mentions quarries at Ardluing and Ardinamar.

By 1800, production of slate in Netherlorn had risen fivefold to 5 million slates a year. When pumping machinery was introduced in the 19th century, the slate workings could be carried down to considerable depths below sea level and production increased. The engine house powered the quarry pumps and ran the railway system to carry finished slates to the pier and remove slate waste. The remains of engine houses can be seen at Cullipool and Toberonochy, while quarry workings and waste are visible in many areas of the island.

Relations between the management and quarriers were often turbulent, and serious accidents were not uncommon. Although the provision of housing for quarriers provided security, conditions of employment and working practices made life very hard. Each quarry crew comprised five slaters who agreed to work together for a year; they in turn subcontracted work to casual and child labour. Quarry workers were paid by the thousand slates sold, but only after the slates had been sold and shipped. In the days of the Marble and Slate Company, workers were paid just twice a year. When money ran out to pay for food and provisions, they were obliged to run up a bill at the Company store, the amounts being literally 'put on the slate'.

By the end of the 18th century a large quantity of slates had been produced but not sold, the workers receiving no payment for their labour. There is no record of what the quarry workers felt about their conditions, or of the resulting poverty of their families. Estate documents give occasional glimpses of considerable

Slate quarriers unloading a bogie at Cullipool (Courtesy: Gilbert Mackay)

Slate splitting at Cullipool quarry in the 1950s (LHG Archives)

discontent. In January 1844 a payment was recorded of £2 10 shillings to the Rural Policeman for the 'expense and trouble' of investigating a riot at Cullipool.

'Boom and bust' characterised the 19th century slate industry. The introduction in 1799 of tax on slate transported by sea and a decrease in the price of slate during the 1840s caused profits to fall significantly. In 1862 the 5th Earl died and in 1866 the Marble and Slate Company of Netherlorn was dissolved. A co-operative of quarrymen was immediately formed, but this failed in 1867, and the various quarries on Luing, and at Easdale and Balvicar, were leased to business consortia.

A revival at the end of the century saw new owners of the quarries at Toberonochy and Cullipool, Messers J & A Maclean, who made significant investments and installed modern machinery. A fine new house was built in each village for the quarry managers, and conditions improved for quarry workers. The new quarry owners agreed to pay workers eight times a year, but they were still only paid when the slates they had made were sold and shipped, and when trade was low they received just a few payments each year. To make matters worse, they were expected to transport the slates to the jetty and load them on boats without payment for this additional work. In July 1893 a boat arrived to collect slates, but the workers at Cullipool refused to start loading until they were paid. After two weeks the quarry owners tried to get workers at Toberonochy to break the strike, seven out of around sixty agreeing to load the slates. Police from Oban turned up, but so did the whole of Cullipool, who convinced the seven Toberonochy men not to proceed. The quarry owners had to capitulate.

By the 20th century large-scale quarrying was in decline, and bankruptcies were common. The owner of the quarries of Toberonochy and Cullipool, J & A McLean, went bankrupt in 1906, while A MacColl, owner of the Port Mary quarry (1) which employed 25 men, went bankrupt in 1911. Production in all quarries ceased during World Wars I and II. In 1937 only the quarries at Toberonochy, Cullipool and Tir na Oig (46) were in production. After WWII the Scottish Slate Company was established, opening operations at Cullipool on Luing and Balvicar on Seil, but in 1966 the two quarries closed for good.

The Earl of Breadalbane also encouraged prospecting for other minerals. In 1730 a 38-year lease was signed to prospect for and mine metals and minerals on his vast estate. Nothing of significance was found on Luing. The lease was eventually made profitable by the discovery and exploitation of significant lead deposits at Tyndrum. In 1789 a prospector of dubious integrity identified lead and other minerals on Breadalbane property, although it seems that no mining of any scale ever took place. Evidence of mineral prospection exists around Luing, in the form of cuttings in the metabasite ridge south of Ardinamar and probe holes in quartz-rich outcrops elsewhere on the island.

Luing's population

Luing's population reflected the changes in economic conditions and the management of the Earl of Breadalbane's estates. In the mid-18th century the population of Kilchattan and Kilbrandon parish was just under 1,500, but by the turn of the century it had increased to over 2,700, around a third of whom lived on Luing. More than a third were connected to slate quarrying.

Luing's population followed the parish trend. A peak was reached in the 1830s and 1840s, and at the time of the 1841 census there were 860 people on Luing. This had fallen to 678 in 1851 and in 1861 to 519, a reduction of 40% in twenty years. Evictions and famine were probably major factors in this population decline, though some may have left of their own accord, seeking better conditions elsewhere. The rents paid by farming tenants had been doubled or more in the early decades of the 19th century, and by the 1830s many were in arrears. Quarry workers were only paid when the slates they had made were sold, leaving them in poverty when sales declined. Between 1846 and 1856 potato famine struck in the Highlands, bringing destitution and pushing many to emigrate.

In 1871 and 1891 the population had risen to 578 and 632 respectively. During this period there were more males than females on Luing, an indication of the resurgence of quarrying, which employed predominantly male workers. Not everyone lived permanently on Luing. The census of 1871 recorded a 'tinkers' camp' of eighteen people in four tents at Bardrishaig (8), including a spoonmaker and three tinsmiths.

By the turn of the century, the population was in decline, dropping to 617 in 1901 and 540 in 1911. Around 90% still spoke Gaelic, which was widely spoken on Luing up to the 1960s. There was a notable drop in the female population from 1901 to 1911, perhaps the result of young women moving away to take up jobs in services and industry in towns and cities. The decline of quarrying after 1910 and the sale of the Netherlorn estate in 1923 marked a new era for Luing.

A brief history of Torsa

The small island of Torsa lies to the north east of Luing, accessible by a causeway at low tide. Like many small islands around Luing, Torsa's name is Norse. By the end of the 9th century AD, the Kingdom of *Dál Riata* had disappeared and Norse settlements were being established in the Hebrides. Norse interest in small islands like Torsa may not have been for their farmland, but for their access to sea routes and other maritime activities. Torsa – Þórisey or Þórðsey (Þórir's island) – may have been a fishing station; with stronger boats, new long-line fishing technology and unfished waters it was boom time for Norse fishing communities.

Another name on Torsa, this time Gaelic, suggests a religious past. Eilean na h'Eaglaise (Island of the Church) is at the northern tip of Torsa, almost an island in its own right (49). It has been suggested that this was a place where secret conventicles were held by Covenanters, but the name may have earlier origins than this.

Torsa lay within a Gaelic-Norse area, which developed in the 12th century into the Kingdom of the Isles under Somerled and his descendents. For most of the period until the early 14th century, Torsa was part of the lands and islands controlled by the MacDougalls, descendants of Somerled's son Dougall. The MacDougalls lost their lands and titles following the Wars of Independence when they opposed Robert the Bruce, their lands passed to their enemies, notably the Campbells and MacDonalds.

In 1313 Torsa was among a grant of lands made by King Robert I to Dougall Campbell of Lochawe, younger son of the leading

Caisteal nan Con overlooking Seil Sound (Courtesy: Dugald MacInnes, ACFA)

Campbell lord Sir Colin, who had been killed by MacDougalls. Torsa lay at the north end of the inland sea route between Islay and the Firth of Lorn, so was strategically important. Later, in 1321, Robert granted Torsa and neighbouring lands to the north of Loch Melfort to a Dugald Campbell in exchange for the service of a galley of twenty-four oars. Possibly the same Dugald Campbell was granted lands in Menstrie, and in 1326 became sheriff of the newly-created Sheriffdom of Argyll. Combined with a judicious marriage, this gave him control of an area from Atholl to Argyll and started the expansion of the Campbell Earls of Argyll.

An indication of the importance of Torsa at this period is the presence of a stone castle, Caisteal nan Con (Castle of the Dogs), on a rock summit on the NE shore of Torsa overlooking Seil Sound (48). Probably built for Campbells in the 15th century, the upper part of the summit is occupied by a small oblong tower-house or hall-house, the lower seaward part by an oblong bailey with a circular tower at the NE corner. The name of the castle has been suggested as indicating a hunting-seat of the Lords of the Isles, or derived from a sobriquet applied by enemies of the owners. Its location, however, suggests a role monitoring, and perhaps taxing, sea traffic using this important Medieval coastal highway.

In 1500 King James IV gave control of the Isles to Archibald Campbell, Earl of Argyll. The superiority of Torsa appears to have remained in the hands of the Earls of Argyll until the late 17th century, when it passed – along with the rest of the Netherlorn estate – to the Campbells of Breadalbane. During the first half of the 16th century Torsa, along with lands on Luing and Shuna, were held from the Campbells by the MacDougalls of Rarey, but these were surrendered by the MacDougalls to the Earl of Argyll in November 1545. Shortly after, on 14 Dec 1545, Torsa was amongst the lands granted by the Earl of Argyll "*in return for service by land and by sea*" to Hector Mòr Maclean of Duart, who had just become the Earl's father-in-law. At the end of the 16th century maps drawn by Timothy Pont show the island as Touirsa, with one settlement.

Early in the 17th century, Torsa was again held under feu by MacDougalls who were closely related by marriage to Campbells. The 17th century was a difficult time for tenants. In the 1630s, after Archibald Campbell had taken over the superiority from his father the 7th Earl of Argyll, tenants were several times issued with eviction notices. As on Luing, the purpose may have been to replace existing tenants with loyalists or to raise rents, or both.

In 1640, MacDougall of Ragray had a three-year steelbow tack for Torsa from the Countess of Argyll. Steelbow tenure was an arrangement whereby the proprietor provided grain, implements and often a sum of money for the incoming tenant who was in return expected to pay a higher rent. The capital provided to MacDougall consisted of 52 bolls of seed oats, 6 bolls of seed bear and 200 merks in money. The rent charged was 32 bolls of meal and 16 bolls of bear, which may be contrasted with the

26 bolls of victual charged in 1666 when there was no mention of steelbow. In 1654 the 8th Earl gave Netherlorn in feu to his younger son, Lord Neil Campbell of Ardmaddy, after whose death in 1692, the estate, including Torsa, was sold to John Campbell, the 1st Earl of Breadalbane.

In the late 17th century estate documents indicate four or five tenants on the island, which was valued at four merklands. Two were Campbells. Changes in the names of other tenants, especially after 1692, appear to reflect the change in island ownership. In 1704 a new name appeared, John MacVarquis and his son, who were probably brought in by the Earl of Breadalbane, given their shared origins in Glenorchy. By 1710 John and son were tacksmen of Torsa, holding the lease and subletting to others, an increase of their status.

In the 1780s, when the Netherlorn estate was reorganised in the name of Improvement it was recommended that Torsa be divided into two distinct 'possessions' and to be occupied by one tenant in each division only. The proposal appears not to have worked, as in the late 1820s and 1830s there were four tenants and one crofter on Torsa. The rent had been more than doubled in 1805 and most tenants appear to have been in substantial arrears in the 1830s. Census records show the population of Torsa at 24 in 1841 (classified as three farming households, 1 cottar family and 1 pauper family). In 1851 it had dropped to 16 and to 9 in 1861. In 1871 the population had risen to 20, sixteen of whom were the families and farm workers of two farmers Donald and James Bell. By 1881 only Donald Bell and his household lived on Torsa, 10 in all. By 1891 it was down to 7 and to 5 in 1911. At the turn of the century, it was described as a 'pleasant fertile single farm of about 250 acres', providing 'excellent pasturage for cattle', its entire surface 'capable of cultivation'.

While farming dominated life on Torsa, its location close to sea-routes and safe anchorages meant close involvement in maritime activities. In 1871 the population at the time of the census included a boatbuilding household. Whether a coincidence or not, the date of 1871 is carved on a rock face above a sheltered anchorage between Torsa and Luing, along with graffiti of several sailing vessels of this period (50). It's possible the graffiti artists were the boatbuilders, or were sailors passing time on the island while they waited for calmer weather. 1871 marked the start of a very strong El Niño, bringing storms and hurricanes.

In 1933 Torsa was sold to Miss Kathryn MacKinnon along with Ardmaddy. After her death in 1938 it was sold to the Struthers family, who still own it. Now Torsa is uninhabited, except for holiday-makers renting the old farmhouse during summer months.

Background reading

For an excellent overview of Scotland's archaeology in different periods and regions including Argyll, read the ScARF and RARFA reports at https://scarf.scot/.

Aimed at adults and older children is 'The Making of Scotland' series of introductory guides to key periods in the prehistory and history of Scotland, published by Historic Scotland and Birlinn. Some of the most relevant titles are included below.

Highly recommended for a detailed understanding rural life in Scotland in the pre-Improvement and Improvement periods are volumes in Alexander Fenton's series on *Scottish Life and Society: A Compendium of Scottish Ethnology*, published by John Donald.

Key books on the history and archaeology of Argyll and the Hebrides are:

Armit, I. ed. 2006. *Beyond the Brochs: Changing Perspectives on the Atlantic Scottish Iron Age*. Edinburgh: Edinburgh University Press

Barclay, G. 1998. *Farmers, Temples and Tombs: Scotland in the Neolithic and Early Bronze Age*. Edinburgh: Historic Scotland and Birlinn

Boardman, S. 2006. *The Campbells 1250-1513*. Edinburgh: Birlinn

Campbell, E. 1999. *Saints and Sea-kings: The First Kingdom of the Scots.* Edinburgh: Historic Scotland and Birlinn

Cavers, G. 2010. *Crannogs and Later Prehistoric Settlement in Western Scotland.* BAR British Series 510

Devine, T. 2006. *Clearance and Improvement: Land, Power and People in Scotland 1700-1900.* Edinburgh: Birlinn

Dodgshon, R. 1998. *From Chiefs to Landlords: Social and Economic Change in the Western Highlands and Islands, c. 1493-1820.* Edinburgh: Edinburgh University Press

Dodgshon, R. 2002. *The Age of the Clans: The Highlands from Somerled to the Clearances.* Edinburgh: Historic Scotland and Birlinn

Dodgshon, R. 2015. *No Stone Unturned: A History of Farming, Landscape and Environment in the Scottish Highlands and Islands.* Edinburgh: Edinburgh University Press

Downham, C. 2007. *Viking Kings of Britain and Ireland: The Dynasty of Ívarr to AD 1014.* Edinburgh: Dunedin

Driscoll, S. 2002. *Alba: The Gaelic Kingdom of Scotland AD 800 – 1124.* Edinburgh: Historic Scotland and Birlinn

Finlayson, B. 1998. *Wild Harvesters: The First People of Scotland.* Edinburgh: Historic Scotland and Birlinn

Foster, S. 2014. *Picts, Gaels and Scots: Early Historic Scotland.* Edinburgh: Birlinn

Fraser, J. 2009. *From Caledonia to Pictland: Scotland to 795.* Edinburgh: Edinburgh University Press

Henderson, J. 2008. *The Atlantic Iron Age: Settlement and Identity in the First Millennium BC.* Abingdon: Routledge

Hingley, R. 1998. *Settlement and Sacrifice: The Later Prehistoric People of Scotland.* Edinburgh: Historic Scotland and Birlinn

MacDonald, C. 1950. *The History of Argyll up to the beginning of the sixteenth century.* Glasgow: Holmes Ltd

McDonald, R. 2008. *The Kingdom of the Isles: Scotland's Western Seaboard c.1100-c.1336.* Edinburgh: Birlinn

McDonald, R. 2019. *The Sea Kings: The Late Norse Kingdoms of Man and the Isles, c.1066-1275.* Edinburgh: Birlinn

McGeachy, R. 2005. *Argyll 1730-1850: Commerce, Community and Culture.* Edinburgh: Birlinn

Maclean-Bristol, N. 1995. *Warriors and Priests: The History of the Clan Maclean, 1300-1570.* East Linton: Tuckwell Press

Maclean-Bristol, N. 1999. *Murder Under Trust: The Crimes and Death of Sir Lachlan Mor Maclean of Duart, 1558-1598.* East Linton: Tuckwell Press

Omand, D. ed. 2006. *The Argyll Book.* Edinburgh: Birlinn

Owen, O. 1999. *The Sea Road: A Viking Voyage Through Scotland.* Edinburgh: Historic Scotland and Birlinn

RCAHMS 1975. *Argyll: An Inventory of the Ancient Monuments, volume 2: Lorn.* Edinburgh: RCAHMS

Ritchie, G. ed. 1997. *The Archaeology of Argyll.* Edinburgh: Edinburgh University Press

Rixson, D. 2000. *The West Highland Galley.* Edinburgh: Birlinn

Shaw, F. 1980. *The Northern and Western Islands of Scotland: Their Economy and Society in the Seventeenth Century.* Edinburgh: John Donald

Withall, M. 2001. *Easdale, Belnahua, Luing and Seil: The Islands that Roofed the World.* Edinburgh: Luath

Woolf, A. 2007. *From Pictland to Alba: 789-1070.* Edinburgh: Edinburgh University Press

Gazetteer of sites

The sites in the gazetteer are numbered, and those numbers are shown on the map. The national grid references are given. More information on some of the sites can be found online on Canmore, the National Record of the Historic Environment (canmore.org.uk), in which case the Canmore ID number is given.

You have the right to access most of the sites on foot and bicycle as long as you act responsibly, respect the environment and follow the Scottish Outdoor Access Code (www.outdooraccess-scotland.scot). Sites that are private are indicated as there is no right of access to houses, gardens or farmyards. The roads on Luing are single track and there is limited car parking so please don't block access to gates and tracks or park in passing places. As Luing's land is farmed and cattle and sheep are outdoors, it is essential that gates are closed, dogs are on a lead at all times, and no litter is left. At certain times of the year there is game shooting. Finally, please do not disturb or damage any historic site. They've survived for centuries, and we hope for many more. If you do find anything of interest, leave it *in situ*, record the precise location and contact Luing History Group – or visit treasuretrovescotland.co.uk which explains what to do.

1
2
Cuan
3

4
Ballachuan
6 5
Cullipool

7
Bardrishaig
8
9
10
12
Ardinamar
11 13

Park 45
43 44
42

14
Leccamore
16 15

47
Achafolla
22
23

46
42
Ardlarach 21
41

17
18
19
Balure

Leccabuy
20

Kilchattan 24
25
40 26
27
Toberonochy

39
38 Blackmill
36 Bay
37 35

29
34 30
33 Ardluing
31

32

Torsa
49
48
50

Places in Gazetteer

Cuan

1. Slate Quarries, Quay and Buildings (NM 748 145)

Cuan point (Courtsey: Chris Whitmore)

19th century slate quarries dominate the northernmost point of Luing west of Cuan ferry, including several deep quarry pits, huge piles and fingers of slate waste, and the remains of quarry buildings, some of which contained engines to drain the pits and drive the railway system to take away finished slate and waste material. The quarry quay, where finished slates were loaded on to boats, is in the inlet immediately west of the ferry slipway. The oldest part, constructed of vertically-set slates, can be seen beside a modern metal jetty used by creel boats. There was also quarrying at Port Mary, immediately south of Cuan point, where there was a small settlement; low stone walls mark two rows of houses (NM 746 138 and NM 745 139) close to the later cattle feeding building.

2. Caves (NM 749 142)

Three caves, two at the bottom of the raised beach and one about 15 metres up from its base, have been used in the recent past, and possibly for many millennia. The higher cave is 4m deep and has a low wall at its entrance and stunning views over the Firth of Lorn. One of the caves at the bottom of the scarp is only 0.6m high, but is 6m deep; slabs placed at its entrance may have given protection against wild winds.

3. Croft (NM 749 137)

Turf-walled croft house at Cuan

An 18-19th century croft with small house and possible barn is located on the hill immediately south of Cuan ferry. Records mention a croft at Cuan in 1731, which may have continued in use until the 1830s. The croft boundary was a stone dyke constructed between outcrops and scarp edges. Inside were areas of cultivation marked by rigs, pasture and a 5m by 3m turf-walled house (NM 74920 13665). A small sub-rectangular structure composed of large boulders may have been used as a winnowing barn or cottar's house (NM 74940 13742), and perhaps in earlier days as a lookout given its sea views north and south-east. The croft is now within an area of native woodland planted in 2021, but open areas have been left around and between the two structures to allow access. Access is through gates in the fence, but please keep the gates closed and avoid any damage to the growing trees.

Ballachuan

4. CROFT (NM 748 134)
South of the track to Port Mary are the remains of another croft, with a sub-rectangular structure, cultivation rigs and a stretch of turf-and-stone wall. The 7m by 4m turf-and-stone-walled structure, with opposing entrances and internal features, is on a raised mound. Records from the end of the 18th century mention a Ballachuan croft, whose tenant in 1804 was Captain Peter Brown.

5. TOWNSHIP AND FARMSTEAD (NM 745 131)

Kiln barn at Ballachuan (Courtesy: Iain Cruickshanks)

Ballachuan was one of Luing's Medieval townships. It was probably held by Macleans in the 14th century, and was occupied until the mid-19th century when it was absorbed into Bardrishaig farm. The remains of stone-walled houses, barns, byres and enclosures from the late 18th and 19th centuries lie around a 20th century sheep fank, constructed of stone from the earlier buildings. Evidence of even earlier buildings can be seen as humps and dips in the ground, their turf walls long gone. The large oval enclosure west of the fank and smaller sub-rectangular enclosure to the south may have early origins too. The remains of a fine stone-built kiln barn for drying grain lie to the south of the fank, away from the settlement to minimise fire risk. In 1730 the two tenants of Ballachuan would have been malting barley as they leased the Change House (inn) at Cuan ferry. One of them also had a lease for fishing; unlike today wild salmon were abundant. Cultivation rigs reveal where the oats and barley were grown. Further south, following a circuitous route from east to west towards Cullipool, is the march dyke between Ballachuan and Bardishaig, constructed of turf and stone and probably dating from the 17th century.

Cullipool

6. Slate quarries, quarry workers' village and church (NM 739 130)

Quarrying started at Cullipool in 1751 and ended in 1965, the last of the Slate Island quarries. By the 1780s there was a scatter of houses surrounded by several quarries, and by 1847 several rows of single-storey cottages had been built by the Marble and Slate Company for quarry workers. One of the earliest cottages is no.8. In 1841 20 slate quarriers lived in Cullipool, but this dropped to just 7 in 1861. The introduction of modern machinery and a revival of the industry led to a jump in Cullipool's population to over 250 in 1871, with 87 working in the quarry. Buildings in the village included engine houses to pump water from the deep quarries and run the railway, a forge and a shop at no.1. Tapped water arrived at Cullipool early in 20th century, several of the water hydrants – with acorn finial and lion's head spout – still surviving. To the north a huge quarry is cut deep into the hill, while in the village there are two now-flooded

Water hydrant in Cullipool village

quarry pits. The Atlantic Islands Centre was built in 2014 on the site of an engine house. Alongside is a one-and-a-half storey house built in 1875 for the quarry manager. Many of the old cottages have slate bothans (sheds) for storage of items such as coal, which was brought ashore from puffers at the quay, transferred in bulk to a coal ree alongside the quarry manager's house, and then distributed in barrows to villagers.

St Peter's Episcopal Church in the 1930s (LHG Archives)

On the hillside behind Cullipool village is St Peter's Episcopal Church (NM 740 130). In the late 18th century, a group of quarriers and their families arrived from Ballachulish. Episcopalians, they established a congregation in 1862 and in 1880 the first St Peter's Episcopal Church was built, an iron building on the site of the current village hall. This was replaced by the stone church in 1894. It closed in 1945 and is now a private holiday house. Behind the church, on the top of a knoll, is a curious enclosure (NM 741 129), its banks formed from natural slate outcrops and the western end of the 17th century march dyke between Ballachuan and Bardrishaig. Called the 'fairy ring' and a favourite spot for children to meet and natter in the past, it may once have been a 'poindfauld' for straying animals. However, its extensive views of the Sound of Luing also suggest a 'watch and ward' function over this busy sea route. After all, Cullipool was once a Norse farm and was within sight of the Medieval fortress of Dun Chonnuill in the Garvellachs.

7. CULLIPOOL QUAY (NM 737 125) AND POWDER HOUSE (NM 739 128)

Cullipool quay, Fladda, Belnahua and Garvellachs in background

South of the village is a substantial slate-built quay. A tramway ran from the quarries to the quayside, small wagons or bogies bringing finished slates and taking back coal to run the steam engines. Improved over time, the quay is still in use as a boat repair yard. Tucked under a cliff behind the houses is a small slate-walled building, which was the 'powder house' where gunpowder for blasting the rock was stored. Opposite the quay is the Old Schoolhouse, now a holiday home. This was North Luing School, built by the School Board in 1895 to provide schooling for children from 5 to 15 years of age. As many as 50 children attended the school in the early 20th century. Later it became an infant and primary school, with twenty pupils and one teacher around 1950. It finally closed in the early 1960s, when slate quarrying at Cullipool was coming to an end.

Bardrishaig

8. FARMSTEAD AND FARMHOUSE (NM 741 123)

Bardrishaig farmhouse, probably late 19th century (LHG Archives)

Bardrishaig (Ardrysack in the 1590s) may once have been a Norse farm. It was one of Luing's Late Medieval townships and an important farmstead in the 19th century. By the early 19th century, the farm was run by the Marques family who were commercial graziers. The farm had expanded to 500 acres, absorbing Ballachuan, where some of the farm workers lived. The farm was doing well and paying good rent to the Earl of Breadalbane, who invested £164 in 1837 to build a fine new farmhouse and another £60 in new dykes and ditches. In 1871 Bardrishaig was farmed by Jemima Marques and her two sons. Much still remains of the 19th century farmstead, including the farmhouse and a bothy, which are private homes so not accessible to the public. Passing by on the road you'll see Tobair nan Camacach (NM 743 122), Well of the Travellers, marked by a post and tin mugs.

Ardinamar

9. SGEIR CARNAICH (NM 751 129, CANMORE ID 22620)

Intertidal cairn, fish trap and march dyke

On the tidal islet of Sgeir Carnaich, at the southern end of the sheltered anchorage between Luing and Torsa, is a large stone cairn, in which ancient oak timbers were embedded. The cairn was investigated for Luing History Group in 2009, carbon-dating of a timber giving a calibrated date of 780-500BC, at the transition between the late Bronze and Early Iron Ages. It was used, though for what purpose is not clear, perhaps by the farming community living on the Ballycastle ridge, which is the same metabasite rock. The intertidal zone here is full of interest: on the southern side of the cairn is a cleared channel suitable for pulling up a boat; close by are the much-eroded remains of a fish trap, visible as a low spread of stones between two outcrops; and over another outcrop south of the cairn is the eastern end of the 17th century march dyke between Ballachuan and Bardrishaig, which runs down beside the burn and across the shore. Over-looking the anchorage to the north of Sgeir Carnaich are the remains of a promontory structure, showing as low turf and stone banks at the end of a prominent basalt dyke (NM 750 132), which may have watched over boats sheltering in the maritime haven between Luing and Torsa.

10. ACHADH DÀ CHALUIM CROFT (NM 749 124)

Possible winnowing barn, view to Ballycastle

High up on Calums' Field, the north-south ridge south of Sgeir Carnaich, are two small structures, probably belonging to a long-abandoned croft. The foundations of an 8m x 4m building, showing as grass-covered boulders, lie in an exposed location with a fine view to Ballycastle; opposing doorways suggest that it might have been a winnowing barn for grain. A little to the north, in a less exposed location at the top of a steep grassy slope showing cultivation rigs, is a 7m x 3m turf structure, possibly the croft house. As population increased during the 18th century, even the most marginal land was used to feed Luing's population.

11. Ballycastle fort and roundhouses (NM 752 120, Canmore ID 22618)

Ballycastle sits atop a hill above Ardinamar, its great stone wall visible from afar and with fine views. The wall is 4m thick and 2m high (it was perhaps 3m high originally) and encloses an area 32m by 18m. Its single entrance passage was once closed with a door and protected by a curve of outer walling, covered by bracken in summer. It may once have been called *Dùnedin*, the name transferred at a much later date to a nearby croft. Classified as an Iron Age dun, only professional investigation would tell how it was used and when. The excavation of similar sites elsewhere in Argyll, including Luing's other hilltop dun at Leccamore, suggests construction in the Iron Age from around 400BC, with possible re-use in the Early Medieval period. There appear to be internal structures, including a possible cistern and oval building, and variations in masonry style may indicate different phases of construction.

Below the entrance on the eastern flanks of the hill are the stone footings of four circular structures, possibly the remains of a small settlement of similar date. One, c.8m in diameter, is close to the dun's entrance on a knoll. Four metres to the south is a second stone structure c.6.5m in diameter, hidden by thorn bushes. Further down the slope is a larger circle of boulders, around 11.5m in diameter. At the bottom, on a knoll above the farm track, is the fourth stone circle, 6.5m in diameter. Nearby is evidence suggesting that people also farmed here: lines of boulders on a stony knoll, which might once have been small enclosures or fields, and which escaped later ploughing (NM 754 121); several 'clearance cairns', their size and shape typical of late prehistoric farming; and a small cellular structure constructed from boulders (NM 753 123).

12. BALLYCASTLE FARMSTEAD (NM 751 120) AND DUNEDIN CROFT (NM 752 127)

ACFA archaeologists recording Dunedin croft

In the 1780s, the farmland of Ardinamar, which until that point had been farmed jointly by several tenants, was divided into two farms and a croft, then in the early 19th century into three farms. Immediately below Ballycastle dun on its west side are the remains of Ballycastle farmstead, one of the three later farms, occupied until the mid-20th century. The farmhouse was demolished in the late 20th century, but still standing is the stone barn with its semi-circular gin platform, on which a horse drove the threshing machine inside. To the north of the farmstead is the kailyard, a rectangular stone-walled enclosure, where vegetables and fruit trees once grew. North of Ballycastle farmstead, on a promontory close to the shore, are the remains of Dunedin croft and one of the 19th century farms. In 1796 the tenant of Dunedin croft was Archibald Campbell, who was allocated the land in return for military service. A boat noust and stone platform by the shore suggest fishing as well as farming. Archibald's croft house was probably not the small building with upstanding stone walls, but was possibly to the north, closer to the shore, where the footings of a 9m x 6m rectangular structure are visible under turf. The remains of more structures are visible on the east and south sides of the upstanding building, including the walls of a kailyard, probably belonging to the 19th century farmstead.

13. ARDINAMAR SETTLEMENT (NM 755 120)

Possible fortified homestead overlooking Ardinamar bay

People have lived at Ardinamar since prehistory. It was one of Luing's Medieval townships and a site of farming, fishing, grain processing, milling and craft activities for centuries. Evidence of

Medieval settlement may be a substantial stone-walled structure, 15m x 11m, on a promontory above the bay (NM 756 122), a possible fortified homestead. Not far to the north are the stone footings of an 8m x 7m oval structure set in a clearing, with signs of terracing and a small enclosure (NM 756 123). In the earliest surviving rentals from 1676, three of Ardinamar's four merklands were leased to 'the miller and smith', while Neill Fisher (Mac-Inniasgar) had the fourth merkland. A long curve of boulders in the bay, visible at low tide, was a fish trap. One of the 17th century tenants may have lived above the bay in a 7m x 4m sub-rectangular turf-walled house (NM 756 121 close to the fence) with attached enclosure. When Ardinamar township was divided into separate farms in the late 18th and 19th centuries, new farm buildings were built in stone. Only a few survive as upstanding buildings. A large barn with semi-circular horse-gin platform is now a private home, as is the double-fronted 19th century farmhouse. The remains of an 18th century mill lie on the south side of the burn (NM 754 119); access is over a stile from the track to Leccamore. Bracken-covered in summer, the mill remains include: a pond with turf banks; a lade cut into the ridge taking water to an overshot mill, whose north wall can be seen through a garden fence; a large corn drying kiln below the track; and a kiln barn lower down beside a stone-walled enclosure.

Large corn-drying kiln at Ardinamar with ACFA and LHG archaeologists

Leccamore

14. Well of the Eye (NM 753 115) and Roundhouses (NM 752 114)

Well of the Eye   *Roundhouse*

Tobar-na-suil (Well of the Eye) is high up on the eastern flank of Leccamore ridge. Look for a group of flat stones on the south side of the Ardinamar-Leccamore boundary fence, below the crumbling dry-stone wall running north-south. According to local folklore the water is good for curing eye diseases. The 'well' is a stone-lined hole above a perched water table or spring, the water collecting above relatively impervious metabasite bedrock. Be sure to replace the cap stone before leaving.

On the western side of the ridge, in a sheltered hollow close to the same fence, are the stone footings of a well-built roundhouse, 7m in diameter, with thick double-walls and a possible annexe off its south side. The roundhouse sits on a levelled platform with a fine view north to Ballycastle dun. A smaller, less visible round structure lies to the south, perhaps a smaller roundhouse. More features lie north of the fence, including small stone structures and a network of field boundaries, the latter easier to spot when dry weather has bleached the moss and turf covering the lines of boulders. Similar sites elsewhere in Scotland suggest this might have been a farming settlement of late Bronze Age date.

15. NORTH LECCAMORE FARMSTEAD (**NM 754 111**)
All that remains of North Leccamore farmstead, created at the end of the 18th century, are the stone footings of several buildings and enclosures. During the 19th century it was a substantial farm; cultivation rigs and seven circular stone stack stands on the eastern edge of the farmstead indicate the importance of grain, which would have been taken to Ardinamar mill for milling. It was in decline during the 20th century, used mainly for sheep, but was occupied until it was demolished in the 1970s. North and west of the farmstead is evidence of earlier farming, notably several substantial turf-and-stone dykes that probably separated the permanent arable areas (infield) from the outfield. An old winding track leads to upland pasture on the ridges to the west.

16. MULTI-CELLED BUILDING AND SHIELINGS (**NM 749 111**)

Drawing of multi-celled
structure (Courtesy: ACFA)

0 ————————— 5m

The foundations of several small huts built crudely from boulders, the largest 6m x 3.5m, lie in rough pasture on a ridge to the west of Leccamore, not far from the end of the winding track. These are thought to have been shielings, the walls and roof probably constructed of turf. They were occupied during summer months when animals had to be kept away from growing crops. The sheep and cattle grazed on species-rich upland pasture and produced milk that was made into cheese and butter. A little to the south, on a level area of ground, is a multi-celled structure built of stone boulders. The 6.5m diameter central cell has three smaller attached cells 3-4m in diameter. There are clear views to both Ballycastle and Leccamore duns and a prehistoric date for its construction is possible. However, multi-celled shielings have been found on other Hebridean islands dating to the 17th century and late Medieval period, some used as dairies. Faint signs of an enclosure on the south-west side of our structure may support this use, enabling the animals to be gathered for milking.

17. Leccamore fort or dun (NM 750 107, Canmore ID 22629)

Southern entrance of Leccamore fort

stairway set in a massive stone wall enclosing an oval area 20m x 13m. It has two entrances, in the southwest and northeast, the latter protected by two deep rock-cut ditches. The southern entrance was barred by a door, the vertical jamb stones and deep bar holes clearly visible. The jamb stone on the entrance passage's east side is made from slate and has fifteen circular indentations – cup-marks – cut into its inner face, typical of late Neolithic and early Bronze Age art. The northern entrance has a corbelled intramural gallery on its west side, with steps leading upwards probably to the top of the dun wall. Leccamore dun was constructed in the Iron Age, most probably after 400 BC and possibly in the early centuries AD, and was again used at the time of *Dál Riata* in the later 1st millennium AD. The late 19th century excavations found great quantities of animal bones under the rubble, suggesting feasting at some point in its life. It's a lovely spot for a picnic, with wonderful views down Luing to the Sound of Jura and east to Shuna and the mainland.

18. SOUTH LECCAMORE FARMSTEAD (**NM 752 104**)
A fine sheep fank marks the location of South Leccamore farmstead, no doubt constructed from the remains of the farm buildings. South Leccamore was created in the 1780s, probably on the site of the earlier Leccamore township although almost no evidence of the latter remains (a stretch of turf-and-stone dyke to the west). In the mid-19th century, the farmstead had four large and two small buildings, but had no inhabitants at the time of the 1871 census.

19. BALURE QUARRY SETTLEMENT (**NM 753 101**)
Of all places on Luing, Balure feels the most mysterious. A line of ruined cottages and buildings face the sea, surrounded by walls of slate waste and several overgrown quarry pits. Balure, which means new settlement in Gaelic, may date from the 1770s when

Balure (Courtesy: Dugald MacInnes, ACFA)

new quarries were opened on Luing. A map of 1787 shows three quarries and four buildings at 'Balure Bay', an anchor indicating a harbour for boats. No doubt boats were pulled up on the shore, loaded with slates at low tide and re-floated at high tide. In the 19th century Balure was a small community of paupers, labourers and craftworkers, including shoemakers, weavers, tailors and carpenters. It is said that the best linen on Luing was made at Balure. Already declining by the 1870s, it was abandoned by the end of the 19th century. Rusting farm equipment and initials carved on stones are the only evidence of Balure's later use.

Leccabuy and Achafolla

20. LECCABUY TOWNSHIP AND FARMSTEAD (NM 747 097)

Leccabuy (or Leckabuy) was one of Luing's late Medieval townships, running from the coast to Achafolla and encompassing Lochan Iliter and a large area of pasture. In the 17th century it was shared by seven or eight tenants. When the townships

Large mound at Leccabuy, view east to Shuna

were reorganised at the end of the 18th century the township was divided into three parts. In a letter of complaint to the Earl of Breadalbane, Alexander Livingston, a tenant of Leccabuy, recalled that not long before 1794 he 'was obliged to demolish the old buildings and build new ones together with an excellent dwelling house all at his own expense'. He reminded the Earl that his family had been in Leccabuy for 200 years. In the early 19th century it was divided again, this time into four farms and three crofts. In 1841 Leccabuy had over 40 inhabitants, including four farming families and one weaving family. Thirty years later there was only one roofed building and three inhabitants. Close to a feeding station and farm track are the slight remains of some of the rectangular buildings, enclosures and houses of the late 18th and 19th century farmsteads of South and Mid Leccabuy. The two farmsteads lay close together, separated only by a dry-stone wall, almost certainly at the site of the pre-Improvement settlement. Immediately south of the wall is a conspicuous mound, with a track winding up to a 16m x 13m rectangular area on top, and stone revetment around most of its perimeter. Though there is no surface evidence of a structure on its summit, its location and character are suggestive of sites used for assemblies and high-status habitations in the Medieval period. There are certainly fine views from the mound over sea routes and harbours, and to the mainland beyond.

21. ACHAFOLLA MILL (NM 742 100) AND SMIDDY (NM 743 099)

A mill and smiddy are known to have existed at Achafolla since the 17th century, and probably existed much earlier, though the location of these buildings is not known. Visible below the road are the upstanding remains of a fine 19th century corn mill, the iron water-wheel still in place and four great millstones inside. Water was drawn from Lochan Iliter, through a now-dry reservoir (Linne Mheadhonach) and finally down a mill lade to drive the overshot wheel. In 1808 £198 was paid by the Earl of Breadalbane for building Achafolla mill, not long after the annual rent for the mill and its croft had been 'augmented' from £16 to £40. The mill building was single storey and constructed mostly of local whinstone. Surrounding the mill was the Miller's Croft, with small house, enclosure and outbuildings. Disused by the 1890s, the mill has been slowing decaying and is now listed as a Building at Risk. Making use of the same flow of water from Lochan Iliter

Ruins of Achafolla mill

was a smiddy. The 19th century stone smiddy building still stands on the east side of the road, today roofed in corrugated iron. The smith lived close by on a small croft – Smith's Croft – a little to the north on the west side of the road.

22. SCHOOL (NM 742 105)

In 1779 the Earl of Breadalbane paid £65 to build a schoolhouse at Achafolla, located close to the forge and mill. It was later much extended and, after a period as a post office, is now a private house. In 1834 a new schoolmaster was in place, renting Leccabuy West Croft to the east, on which a 'comfortable house' was later built (NM 745 101). The 1872 Education Scotland Act brought major changes, including new school buildings (but also the suppression of Gaelic). Land further north was given to the parish School Board to build a new school, schoolmaster's house and playground, which was duly opened in 1877. The double-fronted house was demolished in the 1970s, replaced later by a school garden and small woodland. Built in sandstone and basalt, the 19th century school building survives, albeit without the sound of children following its mothballing in 2020.

School house of Achafolla in 1964 (Courtesy: Ronnie McCord)

23. CHURCH OF SCOTLAND (NM 742 104)
Luing's old parish church fell out of use at the end of the 17th century and after the two parishes of Kilchattan and Kilbrandon were united early in the 18th century a new church was established at North Cuan on Seil, serving both islands (the church is now a private house, but can be recognised by its bell tower). In 1898 the Earl of Breadalbane allocated land at Achafolla for a 'mission station' belonging to the Free Church of Scotland. In 1934 land opposite the school was gifted by the Tyson family of Ardlarach to build a new Church of Scotland. A simple white-painted rectangular building, the church houses a beautifully carved, floor-standing wooden lectern and two wooden offering plates donated by the Latvian owner of a steamship Helena Faulbaums to thank islanders for their rescue efforts when the ship foundered in a storm on Belnahua in 1936. Between the church and school is the War Memorial, a granite obelisk carrying the names of men who lost their lives in the two World Wars.

Kilchattan

24. OLD PARISH CHURCH (NM 744 091, CANMORE ID 22552)
The ruins of the old parish church of Kilchattan stand within a burial ground. One of the earliest parish churches to be built in Lorn, its simple unicameral plan and masonry style – coursed boulders and blocks with panels of pinnings – are typical of buildings of the late 12th century in the northern area of the Kingdom of the Isles. Although in a fragile state, its north, south and west walls remain almost complete. An early Medieval foundation is possible given its dedication to a 6th century Irish saint and the presence of a cross of early type on a stone embedded low in the north wall. In the 13th century graffiti were carved on stones on the southern and northern outer walls, including a

Kilchattan church, view to bay

fleet of boats and two crosses on one, boats with animal heads on their prows on two others, and a square sail and wind-vane on another. The graffiti may depict a passing fleet as the Norwegian and Scots Kings sought – and fought – to establish control of the Isles, perhaps that of King Haakon himself in 1263. In 1404 the Rector of Kilchattan reported to the Pope that the church had been despoiled by a 'powerful layman', perhaps caught up in political or clan conflicts. The church experienced more drama in the 17th century when it was caught up in religious conflicts, and fell out of use as a place or worship by 1690. Since then, it has continued as a place of burial. The earliest known gravestone, a recumbent slab inside the church, carries a date of 1680. Over 700 gravestones lie around the church and in a new graveyard to the side. Their fascinating history is told in the Kilchattan Kirkyard book, which records the stones and inscriptions following a survey in 2003-2005 by Luing History Group.

25. KILCHATTAN TOWNSHIP AND FARMS (NM 744 091)

Though it's now hard to believe, until the mid-19th century

Kilchattan church stood at the centre of a substantial settlement. Kilchattan was one of Luing's late Medieval townships, more valuable than most other townships at 6 merklands, probably reflecting the extent of its arable land. Rentals from the 1660s and 1670s show it 'in tack' to a Stewart, not a local name, unlike the tenants of Luing's other townships. The Earl of Argyll's wife was a Stewart, so it's possible the lease of this valuable township was given to a family follower. After the estate's purchase by the Earl of Breadalbane in 1692, Kilchattan was shared by multiple tenants, sometimes as many as eight, including several Campbells. At the end of the 18th century the township was divided into three farms, each farm with two tenants, and by 1830 a croft had also been created. An 1847 estate map shows 25 buildings around the church. Based on the occupations of people living there in 1841, the buildings included farm houses and farm buildings, a shop, and the small houses of agricultural workers, weavers, cottars and paupers. Shortly afterwards the settlement was emptied, to make way for a 'model farm', the departure of tenants so abrupt that two of them left behind pictures, which the Most Noble Marquess of Breadalbane paid 10 shillings to have valued in 1848. By 1871 only one household lived at Kilchattan, the overseer of Kilchattan model farm.

26. Kilchattan Model Farm (NM 745 089)

Known locally as the Square, Kilchattan farm was built in 1853, at the forefront of agricultural developments of the time. The model farm included two houses, a barn range, huge byre, stables and piggeries, built in the best Luing whinstone, the walls packed inside with slate. A huge slurry tank was built close to the byre, a powerful engine pumping the slurry out to nearby fields. A threshing machine was run by a water wheel, the water coming all the way from Lochan Iliter to Achafolla, then along a lade to a holding tank north of the steading. The lade can still be seen running through the field west of Kilchattan graveyard. Though the water wheel and many of the farm buildings have gone, remnants of the fine 19th century stone steading remain. Nowadays the Square is the hub of Ardlarach farm, famous for its Luing cattle, with houses for farm workers, byres and huge barns to store silage grown in surrounding fields.

Toberonochy

27. TOBERONOCHY SLATE QUARRIES AND VILLAGE (**NM 749 086**)

Toberonochy takes its name from a well, Tobar Donnachaidh (Duncan's Well), which still exists by the shore. The village grew up around a slate quarry, first opened here in 1766. A 1787 map shows two quarries but no settlement at 'Kilchattan Bay', but by 1841 the census recorded 46 households, predominantly slate workers. After the creation of the model farm in the 1850s and clearing of tenants from Kilchattan and Ardluing, Toberonochy's population included the families of farm workers. By 1871 it had dropped to 36 households, with far fewer quarry workers than thirty years previously. The slate industry revived and employment at Toberonochy quarry reached a peak of over 50 workers in the 1890s. Pumping machinery enabled the slate workings to be carried down to considerable depths, as evidenced by the huge water-filled quarry pit behind the quarry-workers' cottages.

Toberonochy village

On the east side of the quarry were engine houses, one of which drained the quarry workings and lifted out slate, others running the trams that took the slate away. Two great fingers of waste slate extended from the shore, a tramway on each depositing the waste. Boats called in at the jetty to take away finished slates and leave behind their ballast. The ballast is said to have included soil from Ireland, which was added to villagers' vegetable gardens. South of Toberonochy (NM 748 082) are the remains of the powder house, a small slate building where gunpowder for blasting the rock was stored, well away from the settlement. Quarrying ended in the early 20th century, and today Toberonochy is peaceful, known for its green-fingered residents and colourful gardens, still benefiting from the rich Irish soil.

Ardluing

28. Islet by Eilean an Atha (NM 748 072, Canmore ID 22556)

Tidal islet at entrance to bay

On a rocky islet in a bay overlooking Shuna Sound is a D-shaped structure composed of a low but thick stone wall enclosing an area roughly 18m x 12m. There are signs of an entrance on the south side and a short spur of external wall on its south-east corner. It has been classified as a 'dun' by official surveys, but shares few characteristics with most Iron Age duns. Its shape and location – opposite 'Watch island' (Shuna), overlooking a major Medieval seaway, and protecting a shallow bay ideal for drawing up longboats and galleys – suggest a later date, though all theories are speculative given the absence of diagnostic features and dating evidence. The islet is easily accessible at low tide from the western side of the bar, crossing to a sand bar extending from the islet.

29. Captain Campbell's Cottage (NM 743 071)

Lintel of Capt. Campbell's Cottage

The remains of a small stone-built house sit on a rise to the west of the Ardluing track, backed by a cattle-feeding station. An inscription on the slate lintel over the front door reads 'Built by Capt. John Campbell 91st Reg. MRc. 1816'. The 91st Regiment was raised for the Duke of Argyll and fought during the French Revolutionary and Napoleonic Wars. In 1818 Capt. Campbell married Elizabeth Stevenson, whose family owned Belnahua slate quarry island and were property developers in Oban. It seems they had little more than a decade to enjoy the fine house. In 1829 Capt. Campbell owed £20 rent, which was 'in course of collection from sales under sequestration', his financial difficulties due perhaps to Elizabeth's family, some of whom were deeply in debt at this time, mostly from the Belnahua quarry. They seem to have stayed in the parish and were later buried in Kilchattan, a headstone marking their grave. The house at Ardluing continued to have military connections, as a new lease for land at this location was signed in 1929 by Captain D. MacInnes. The house, repaired in 1837 and patched with brick in later years, appears to have been used – though possibly for farm purposes – until the 1940s, but was unroofed by the 1950s.

30. Mid Ardluing 'Old Town' and farmstead (NM 744 068)
At eight merklands, Ardluing was double the value of most late Medieval townships on Luing, and was probably farmed as two separate townships. One of them was at the location of the later Mid Ardluing farmstead, as a report of 1796 referred to this as the site of 'the Old Town'. A large stone-walled sheep fank now marks its location. South, west and north of the fank lie the footings – some of turf, others of stone – of enclosures, buildings and structures of varying shapes and sizes. Some of the turf structures

ACFA and LHG volunteers recording Mid Ardluing

may belong to the late Medieval settlement, for instance a substantial bow-sided structure on a raised platform and a sub-rectangular building set in a small enclosure south of the fank. A sinuous and substantial turf-and-stone dyke running almost the length of Ardluing and passing close to this settlement may also date to this period; it may have been a head dyke between the infield (arable) to the east and outfield (pasture) to the west. In 1785 Ardluing was divided into four farms, one of which was Mid Ardluing. The old structures were replaced with rectangular enclosures and three-compartment buildings with stone footings, some visible to the north of the fank. In the later 19th century, Ardluing was turned over to cattle and sheep; linear pits may have been sheep dips and some of the turf structures on the hill east of the fank might have been used for stock management. In 1871 the only household recorded as living at Ardluing was a shepherd and his wife and seven children.

31. South Ardluing farmstead (NM 745 068)

Created in the 1780s, the remains of South Ardluing farmstead show clearly in the ground, including enclosures and three long buildings each with three or four compartments, which were houses with attached barns and byres. The fields around were drained, ploughed and cultivated, as evidenced by the rigs and drainage channels. On the south-west edge of the farmstead runs a particularly impressive section of the circuitous turf-and-stone dyke running down Ardluing. South Ardluing was lived in for just seventy years before its population was cleared in the 1850s.

32. Promontory earthwork (NM 743 057)

On top of a prominent outcrop with extensive views down the Sound of Jura and around is a low barrel-shaped earth bank roughly 9.5m x 6m. A gulley protects it on its north side, precip-itous slopes on the others. Not marked on any map or recorded in any document, its location and character suggest a lookout, watching over a significant sea route and a historic division between mainland Argyll and the Isles. It overlooks a tidal island, the dense rig showing how heavily it was cultivated in the past.

33. Promontory earthwork (NM 737 066, Canmore 22555)

View of promontory earthwork across Sound of Luing to Scarba

On a rocky promontory in the west coast of Ardluing is a substantial trapezoidal earthwork, 16m x 10.5m. It is well suited for defence, with precipitous drops on its seaward side and a deep gulley on its eastern side. The entrance in the north is protected by a ditch and 20m long rampart. No structures are visible in the interior. There are far-reaching views south to the Sound of Jura and north to the Firth of Lorn, and facing the promontory to the west is the channel (and Grey Dog tidal race) between the islands of Scarba and Lunga. The site's date is unknown, but – like other promontory structures around Luing – its location and earth construction suggest that it could be Medieval, with a role monitoring – and perhaps controlling – an important sea route through the Sound of Luing.

34. West Ardluing farmstead (NM 741 069)

Like South Ardluing, West Ardluing farmstead was created in the 1780s and continued until the 1850s. The farmstead was composed of four long structures, three with two compartments and one with three compartments, most probably byre-houses. A large, 50m x 16m, enclosure to the east was possibly for stock, as it seems too exposed for a kailyard. The enclosure's westerly bank forms part of the circuitous turf-and-stone dyke dividing Ardluing.

A short distance to the north-west (NM 740 070) is another house with annex and yard, the house scooped into the ground surface and the yard with turf banks and external ditch. Still in use in the 1840s, it's possible this site started life earlier than the late 18th century; small turf-walled houses with attached enclosures or yards were a feature of pre-Improvement settlements, as seen at Ardinamar and Mid Ardluing.

35. Cave and rock shelter (NM 737 079)

Close to the base of a former sea cliff is a 5m deep cave with signs of boulders embedded in its floor. A little to the north, half way up the cliff, is a very large rock shelter, under which is a great deal of accumulated material bordered by an earthen bank. An accretion on the back wall of the rock shelter containing limpet shells probably occurred when sea levels were very different to today. With extensive views it's possible the cave and shelter have provided protection from the elements for millennia, given the many examples of early prehistoric occupation of such places in the area.

Blackmill Bay

View south to Blackmill Bay and Sound of Jura

36. Promontory structure (NM 733 083)

On a promontory above the current settlement is an interesting earthen structure that could be one of Luing's Medieval 'watch and ward' defences. A small squarish structure 5m x 4.5m sits inside a 10m x 8m earthen bank, the promontory further protected by a cross-bank and ditch. With extensive views down the Sound of Jura and over the Sound of Luing to the Medieval fortress of Dun Chonnuill, it would have been a perfect place to watch for approaching longboats or galleys, and perhaps light a beacon to warn others of imminent threats.

37. Blackmill Bay slate quarries and settlement (NM 732 082)

Blackmill Bay is now a quiet corner of Luing, but back in time it was a hive of activity. In the 18th century there were slate quarries, a croft and a busy mill. In 1841 over twenty households lived there. Steamers called in to offload cargo, waiting passengers could buy goods in the shop and enjoy a drink at the inn. Slate quarrying lasted at most a hundred years. The 1841 census listed twenty-one households, but only one person was a slate quarrier.

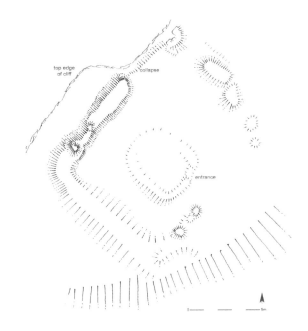

Drawing of promontory structure at Blackmill Bay (Courtesy: ACFA)

There were two shoemakers, a tailor, a merchant and a large farming household, but fourteen households were classified as 'cottar and labourer' or even more unfortunate as 'cottar pauper'.

38. Pier and ticket office (NM 732 083)

In 1841 one resident of Blackmill Bay was the 'steamboat agent'. Paddle-steamers started operating from the Clyde to the Hebrides and North West Scotland via Oban and the Crinan Canal in the 1820s, calling in at Blackmill Bay. Nearby was a 'change house' providing travellers with ale, spirits and refreshments. In 1848 the new tenant of the inn, Alexander MacPhail, and a boatman were killed while conveying four passengers out to a steamer by rowing boat. Accusations of recklessness were made against the steamboat crew, who only a week earlier had caused a quarry boat

Relaxing at the pier in the 1930s (Courtesy: Ronnie McCord)

loaded with slates to sink at Easdale. A new pier was built in the early 1890s, enabling passengers and cargo to be transferred more safely between land and boat. Over 50 men, mostly from Cullipool, contributed their labour free of charge to building the new pier, four of them providing their horse and cart. The first World War and then the motor bus in the 1920s brought an end to travel by steamer between Oban and Crinan. In the 1930s the Pier was a place to relax and enjoy the view. Only remnants of the pier remain, but the Ticket Office and Waiting Room still stands, no longer painted white and without its chimney, and listed as a 'Building at Risk' by Historic Environment Scotland.

39. MILL (NM 734 086)

The first record of Blackmill Bay is from 1766, when rent increases for the 'Croft and Mill of Blackmill Bay' are mentioned. A Black Croft is mentioned in 1735, so it seems likely that the croft and mill were in existence before the 1750s. It was probably a horizontal mill. A report to the Earl of Breadalbane on the state of Luing's mills in 1796 describes the Black Miln as being in *'tolerable repair'* and the recommendation was to allow it to

Remains of mill, broken millstone in grass

remain '*as long as it will stand, or as long as the miller chooses to keep it up ar his own expence; which will probably be longer than if it was to be repaired at your Lordship's*'. The mill continued in use but a report of 1814 complained about the mill dam and surrounding 'quagmire', and recommended that the mill and dam be demolished. Further work on the water course was carried out in the 1830s, but by 1847 the mill was out of use. The remains of the mill can still be seen between the bridge and the shore; a broken millstone, stone walling on the sides of the water channel, the cutting in the rock outcrop, and humps and bumps in the ground where the buildings were located.

Ardlarach

40. ARDLARACH HOUSE AND NETHER ARDLARACH FARM (NM 735 089, CANMORE ID 79984)

Nether Ardlarach was one of Luing's late Medieval townships, though no evidence of a settlement of this period remains. In the 17th century the tenants were MacDougalls, but all changed in 1709 when a 7-year tack for the whole farm was given to Robert Campbell, formerly tenant of Bardrishaig, whose brother was chief of the Campbells of Lochdochart, a minor clan of the Campbells of Breadalbane. In the 1730s the tenancy was shared between two Campbells and a Tait, but by the end of the 18th century Nether Ardlarach was back in the hands of MacDougalls. In 1787, at the time of Improvement, a new farmhouse was built with two storeys and a slate roof, then extended in the 19th century. In 1834, when Allan MacDougall, a commercial grazier, held the tenancy, it was the finest house on Luing. Twenty servants, farm labourers and cottars worked and lived on the farm in 1841. In 1848 Allan's tenancy was ended, and Lower Ardlarach was absorbed into the model farm at Kilchattan. The houses and farm at Ardlarach are private and cannot be visited.

41. Dùn Ablaich (NM 738 097, Canmore ID 22554)

Dun Ablaich

This is an intriguing site, an earthwork on top of a rocky knoll rising out of an extensive marshy area north of Ardlarach farmhouse. Around the edge of the knoll is an earthen bank, enclosing an elliptical area 27m x 12m. A possible entrance lies at the N end, approached by a path up a slope. Though rough grass covers the interior, lines of humps and a possible platform suggest internal features. The survival of its description as a 'dùn' (a fort) and its name Ablaich (pronounced Doonevalich) indicates a site of some importance, maintained in local memory and records. Its name is difficult to interpret; it could refer in Gaelic to carrion, or more prosaically in Norse to 'stream of the main farm'. Not far to the north is Achafolla or 'field of blood'. A letter of 1853 to the Earl of Breadalbane's factor mentions 'deer horns' from Kilchattan Moss, perhaps the remains of carrion. Running through the Moss is the burn carrying water from Lochan Iliter, which drains to Blackmill Bay. Before extensive drainage, the Moss was partly under water; the name of a field to the south is tantalisingly called 'Castleloch'. The dùn can be reached from the south, walking up the side of the main drainage channel.

42. Upper Ardlarach or Park (NM 739 112) and Mid Ardlarach (NM 739 102)

Upper Ardlarach was one of Luing's late Medieval townships, in existence by the 14th century, when the 'lands of Ardlarach' were granted by the Lord of the Isles to the Macleans of Duart. It was evidently of strategic importance, overlooking the Sound of Luing and within reach of the great fortress of Dun Chonnuill. When the pre-Improvement farms were reorganised in 1787, Upper Ardlarach was divided in two. A map from that time indicates that the old settlement was renamed Mid Ardlarach and a new farm of Upper Ardlarach created further north. Mid Ardlarach was still a farm in the 1840s, but was abandoned by the 1870s, the land perhaps absorbed into the model farm or Upper Ardlarach. The footings of Mid Ardlarach's buildings, enclosures and a corn drying kiln can be seen under turf.

By 1829 Upper Ardlarach had itself been divided in two, one part called Park. Rather than move house, a winding stone dyke,

Park farmstead in 1930s (LHG Archives)

making the most of natural outcrops and ridges, was built to mark the division; this ran through the middle of the old farmstead, leaving Park steading on higher ground to the east and Upper Ardlarach on lower ground to the west. By 1871 there was only one farming family living there. Park was still occupied in the 1930s, with a small single-storey farmhouse, byre and barn. The farmhouse and byre were demolished in the 1970s, but the barn still stands with a new roof.

43. COTTAR'S HOUSE (**NM 739 114**)

Alongside the track to the north of Park are the remains of a small house, possibly belonging to a farm worker. Sub-rectangular, barely 5m x 3m, and on a raised area, the house's turf walls sat on stone footings, which are clearly visible at the track end. There is evidence of an annex on one side and a small enclosure cut into the slope at the back. Despite being small and basic, it's possible such a dwelling was occupied into the 19th century, though an earlier – pre-Improvement – date is possible.

Eroding end of turf-walled house on stone foundations

44. STONE CIRCLE (NM 742 133)

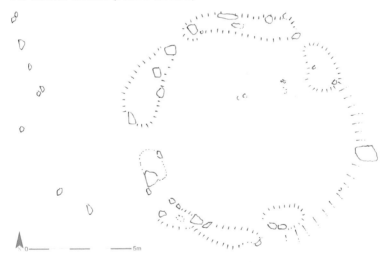

Drawing of circular structure (Courtesy: ACFA)

10m in diameter, a circle of boulders with an entrance on the south-east marks the site of a possible roundhouse, which may be of late Bronze Age or Iron Age date. The circle appears to sit on a levelled area, and a large recumbent boulder lies outside the entrance. A linear arrangement of slate boulders a few metres to the west may indicate an associated enclosure or field boundary. Although on a flat area of ground it's not easy to see; in summer it's covered by rushes and can be very muddy when wet.

45. FORTIFIED HOMESTEAD (NM 741 116)

View of structure at Park, looking west toward Dun Chonnuill

Eighteen metres in diameter and constructed of turf and stone, this large circular structure sits on a level ridge with extensive views west. The anchorages and shore south of Cullipool and the fortress of Dun Chonnuill are in clear sight. This is a complex and possibly multi-phase structure, and may have suffered from cattle disturbance or ploughing or both, particularly on its eastern side. Huge boulders show at the base of the outer bank.

On the western side there is evidence of a double wall with internal cell or passage. There appears to be an entrance on the northern side, marked by particularly massive boulders and an intramural cell, beyond which the entrance passage does a dogleg into the central area. The existence of an internal structure, possibly sub-rectangular, is suggested by lines of stone walling visible at the western end. Running from the north-west corner is a stretch of wall constructed of large slates, bedded vertically

East wall of circular structure at Park showing large boulders

in the ground. To the east is a slate outcrop on which there is a considerable quantity of slate mixed with earth, though whether this is a dump of material or is hiding a structure is unclear. A prominent turf-and-stone dyke runs east and north of the structure, enclosing an area of cultivated land. Although some aspects of the circular structure might be very early in date – perhaps a large prehistoric roundhouse – other aspects bear similarities to Medieval secular seignorial buildings in western Argyll dating to the 13th century and later, which are characterised by the re-use of late prehistoric sites, constructions in earth and timber, and strategic locations controlling arable land and routeways. The structure is easier to see in winter when bracken is low. Constructed in earth it is relatively fragile, so care should be taken when visiting the site to avoid dislodging stones or damaging earth banks.

46. Tir na Oig slate quarry (NM 733 103) and Coffin Road (NM 732 099)

Engine at Tir na Oig
(Courtesy: John Rahtz)

Little is known about this slate quarry, located below a steep cliff on the Ardlarach coast, huge fingers of slate waste extending like a hand from the cliff. It's likely that it was in operation only from the 1920s until just after WWII. The rusted remains of the tramway, track and wagons can still be seen on the quarry slopes and right at the top is the almost-complete engine. The engine is a 1922 air compressor that helped drill holes for explosives or wedges to split the slate rock; the machine revolutionised quarrying by replacing labour-intensive and arduous hand drilling. A small slate building at the foot was probably the powder house. In 1934 a young worker, Gilbert May, died in an accident at the quarry. The boatman for Fladda lighthouse, Hugh MacLachlan, used to ferry workers from Cullipool to the quarry jetty, linked to the quarry by a tramline. It can be a muddy walk to get there and a scramble up the huge fingers of slate waste, but it's atmospheric and there are fine views west. A little to the south of Tir na Oig is Coffin Road, a grass-covered track climbing gently up the slope of the old sea cliff. This was the final journey of people who had died on Belnahua and other offshore islands, their coffins carried up the Road and over to Kilchattan for burial.

47. EASAN FROGACH OR FAIRY WELL (NM 743 109)

On the east side of Luing's main road through the Dubh-Leitir glen is Easan Frogach, the waterfall of the bewitched, tucked in undergrowth. A burn runs down a hard felsite sill and at its foot is a mossy mound in which fairies were thought to live. It was the custom for passers-by to pull a thread from their garments and lay it on the mound as a peace

Easan Frogach

offering. Recently the fairies added a small door to the mound, not to be opened. Rising sharply on the east side of the glen is the long ridge of Binnein Furachail, the hill of watchfulness, though whether this was to spot fairies or protect people and livestock hidden in the dark glen is not known.

Torsa

48. CAISTEAL NAN CON (NM 765 138, CANMORE ID 22631)

The remains of a Medieval stone castle occupy a prominent rocky outcrop on the north-east coast of Torsa. A small oblong tower-house, roughly 14m x 9m, stood at the landward end; and at the lower seaward end there was an oblong bailey, 16m x 11m overall, with a circular tower in the north-east corner. The castle entrance was probably on the south side of the bailey. The buildings are very ruinous and covered in vegetation. A rocky inlet to the north-east of the castle could have served as a boat landing.

Caisteal nan Con

Probably built by Campbells in the 15th century, the castle's name has been translated as Castle of the Dogs, its use suggested as a hunting lodge. It's likely the castle played a role monitoring and perhaps taxing sea traffic passing through Seil Sound, and was built as a statement of power and aspiration by an ambitious Campbell. It seems to have been out of use by the end of the 16th century.

49. FARMSTEAD (NM 765 137)

Until the late 19th century there were two farming settlements on Torsa. One was at the southern end, where the old farmhouse is now a holiday let, the other was at the northern end, in the south-east corner of Eilean na h'Eaglaise (Island of the Church), separated from Torsa by a shallow channel. There's no evidence of an early church here, but it may be hidden under later buildings. The site of the settlement is marked by a 20th century sheep fank and dip, built in stone from walls of the 19th century farmstead. The main part of the fank was once a small barn, with opposing doorways and triangular holes in the walls ensuring ventilation. The footings of old buildings and walled enclosures surround

Barn and Fank, view south to Caisteal nan Con

the fank. Evidence of earlier occupation may be indicated by a low curving bank running under later walls. A corn drying kiln is built into the sides of an outcrop a little to the east. Cultivation rigs cover Torsa, an interesting patchwork of small areas of narrow, hand-dug rigs and larger areas that have been ploughed. Incorporated in a wall footing to the north of the barn/fank is a broken knocking stone used for pounding barley and another knocking stone lies outside the southern farmhouse, further proof of Torsa's grain-growing past.

50. Boat graffiti (NM 757 130, Canmore ID 304894)
Striking boat graffiti cover a vertical rock face on the south-west coast of Torsa, overlooking a sheltered anchorage. Several sailing vessels and a hand have been carved into the rock, along with dates including 1871 and 1929. Under the rock face is a narrow

Boat graffiti on Torsa

ledge, which is said to have been a good spot for fishing. In 1871 a boatbuilding household lived on Torsa. As this was also a year of storms and hurricanes, the graffiti artists may have been island residents or visiting sailors waiting for calmer weather.